Be it my 1st or 15th

Am I Ready for A(nother) Puppy or Dog?

(What you should know before you open your wallet)

Karen Peak

Be it my 1ˢᵗ or 15ᵗʰ

Am I Ready for A(nother) Puppy or Dog?

(What you should know before you open your wallet)

By Karen Peak

Copyright, Legal Notice, Disclaimer and such things I have to put in.

This publication is protected under the US Copyright Act of 1976 and all other applicable international, federal, state and local laws, and all rights are reserved, including resale rights: if you have an electronic copy, you are not allowed to give or sell this eBook to anyone else. If you received this publication from anyone other than having purchased it, you've received a pirated copy. Please contact us via e-mail and notify us of the situation.

Please note that much of this publication is based on personal experience and anecdotal evidence. Although the author and publisher have made every reasonable attempt to achieve complete accuracy of the content, they assume no responsibility for errors or omissions. Also, you should use this information as you see fit, and at your own risk. Your particular situation may not be exactly suited to the examples illustrated here; in fact, it's likely that they won't be the same, and you should adjust your use of the information and recommendations accordingly.

Any trademarks, service marks, product names or named features are assumed to be the property of their respective owners, and are used only for reference. There is no implied endorsement if we use one of these terms.

All pictures are property of Karen Peak and West Wind Dog Training (www.WestWindDogTraining.com) and The Safe Kids/Safe Dogs Project (www.SafeKidsSafeDogs.com).

Finally, use your head. Nothing in this book is intended to replace common sense, legal, medical or other professional advice, and is meant only to inform and entertain the reader.

Copyright © 2012 Karen Peak, West Wind Dog Training. All rights reserved worldwide.

Published 2012
First Edition
Printed in the USA
ISBN # 978-0615597812

Dedications

This is dedicated to my parents, mentors, colleagues and friends I have made over the years who have helped me grow and continue to grow in the world of dogs. There are too many of you to list!

To my husband who lovingly puts up with me and the critters, the hair, the wet dog smell, the cats, the myriad of other critters that have graced our lives and other things: thank you.

My children and dogs who taught me that by becoming a parent, I have become a more observant canine professional and that by being a canine professional, I have become a better parent.

 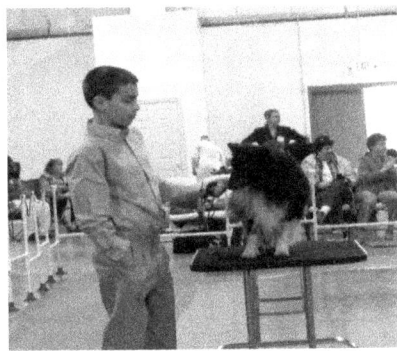

And to one special client, years ago, whose goofy, active pup had her not quite at the end of her rope. Years later, they are competing in Rally Obedience and are a Pet Therapy team at local facilities. Thank you for listening and following my recommendations when our classes were complete. When I grow saddened by clients who can do it, but choose not, I think of you and your goofy Lab and all you have accomplished.

(And big thanks to GB for taking the time to edit this!)

Foreword

Thank you for choosing this book. Let me take a moment to introduce myself: I began working formally with my first dog, Muffin, a blue merle Shetland Sheepdog, in 1982. I have a background that includes some Competitive Obedience, Rally Obedience, Agility and Conformation competitions. I have volunteered in various capacities with rescue groups. I am a member, webmaster and educational liaison for dog clubs. I have had the pleasure of knowing some wonderful breeders, judges, competitors, veterinarians, trainers and behaviorists throughout my life. All these experiences shaped what I have become and continue to help me determine the paths I take.

As I grew as a trainer, I began looking closer at how many of my clients ended up with the situations they called me to address. For some, it was a case of the owners acquired a puppy or dog and had no idea what they were getting into. They were unprepared. Others were prepared but did not choose a good match. They were ready for a dog, just not the dog they chose.

There are many books on the market about what to do once you get a dog. There are not as many that address what you should consider before you get a dog. I wanted to write a short book designed to get someone considering a dog to pause a moment, think and reflect: is this what I should be doing? Am I ready for a dog? Have I checked my sources? Am I making the best possible choice for my family at this point in time? Have I thought of the next fifteen to eighteen years?

If I can get one person to stop, think, evaluate carefully what is being considered and make the best choice possible, then this effort has been worth it. If you are reading this, then you are taking that first important step many forget: close self-evaluation. Thank you!

Table of Contents

CHAPTER 1 - WHY DO I WANT A DOG?   1

- COMPANIONSHIP   1
- PROTECTION   3
- CHILD/CHILDREN ASKED FOR   5
- RECOMMENDED BY ANOTHER   7
- WORKING PARTNER   8
- VANITY   9
- IMPULSE   10
- WHY DO I WANT A DOG?   10

CHAPTER 2 - AM I READY FOR A DOG?   11

- TIME COMMITMENT   11
- HUMAN MEDICAL ISSUES   13
- COST   15
- HOUSING   18
- LIFESTYLE   20
- GROOMING   21
- EXPERIENCE   21
- YOUR FUTURE   22
- GOLDEN YEARS   23
- AGREEMENT   23
- LEGAL/MISCELLANEOUS   24
- AM I READY FOR A DOG?   25

CHAPTER 3 - WHAT TYPE OF DOG IS BEST FOR ME?   27

- PUREBRED OR CROSSBRED   27
- PUPPY OR ADULT   30
- WHAT BREED IS BEST?   31
- HOW HIGH IS HIGH ENERGY?   33
- AM I EXPERIENCED ENOUGH FOR THIS DOG?   34
- CAN I PHYSICALLY MANAGE THE DOG I WANT?   35
- WHAT IS THE BEST DOG FOR CHILDREN?   36
- WHAT IS THE BEST DOG FOR A HOME WITH OTHER PETS?   40
- IS MY CURRENT PET READY FOR A NEW PUPPY OR DOG?   42
- WHAT AGE DOG SHOULD I ADD?   44
- TWO MAY NOT BE BETTER THAN ONE   45

Table of Contents

CHAPTER 4 - WHERE AND HOW SHOULD I CHOOSE MY DOG?	47
RESCUES	47
BREEDERS	58
PET SHOPS	63
CHAPTER 5 - WHAT SHOULD I DO BEFORE I BRING MY DOG HOME?	65
BASIC SUPPLIES	65
FINDING A VETERINARIAN	66
FINDING A TRAINER	67
MISCELLANEOUS SERVICES	72
CHAPTER 6 - SPECIAL NOTES ON SPECIAL NEEDS DOGS	77
BEHAVIORAL	77
PHYSICAL	81
MEDICAL	83
CONCLUSION	87
RESOURCES	89
RECOMMENDED AUTHORS	91

x

CHAPTER ONE

WHY DO I WANT A DOG?

Why do you want a dog? If you are like most of my clients or people who contact me while they are researching dogs, your reasons are probably one of the following:

    Companionship
    Protection
    Children asked for
    Recommended by another
    Working partner
    Vanity
    Impulse (have a tough time walking past stores without buying something)

The first place we have to begin when we are considering a dog is why we desire a dog. This will help you determine if a dog is really what you should be considering in your life at this point and whether a dog will continue to suit your needs in the future. Before you commit to a purchase or adoption, take a moment and look at each common reason:

COMPANIONSHIP

The majority of potential dog owners contact me regarding companion dogs. Some want a dog to enhance their lives while others are trying to make up for a broken relationship or to try to replace a feeling of something lost. Which one are you?

I associate acquiring a dog to having a child. Though we are different species, there are analogies to be made. There is a lot of preparation, long term commitment and financial considerations. If you are not ready for the responsibility of a creature that requires training, a significant amount of daily interaction, socializing, "potty" training and education, should you be adding a life to your home at this point? Being a generally social species, dogs are a natural for integrating into a family, if you are serious about doing the work. However, when the owner fails to hold up his end of the relationship and perform meaningful, educational interactions, a dog will often develop problems. If you do not put in the time and meaningful effort to a child, the child stands a greater chance of going astray. The more positive experiences and education your dog has, especially as a puppy, the better off he will be as he grows.

A companion dog must learn to become a companion. This means learning how to live with a species that has a different set of behaviors, different vocalizations and body language. I have heard it stated by many dog trainers and behaviorists that your puppy must meet and greet one hundred people by the age of twelve weeks. How is this possible? It is not very difficult when you break this goal down: you take your puppy to five new places a week and meet five new people at each place; your puppy will meet 100 new people in four weeks (5x5 = 25x4 = 100).

You get a pup at 8 weeks and this gives you four weeks to meet this goal. My only concern is health risks to a puppy before the puppy vaccines are complete (generally around 12 weeks of age). In areas like mine where Parvo Virus is an issue, you have to be cautious. I would not be taking a puppy to places where many dogs frequent such as pet supply stores and dog parks at this point: however, there are still things you can do at home. Bring in as many people as you can to your house to play with the puppy every day. Have him meet the letter carrier, any delivery people, and even those annoying door to door sales people can be put to use before you tell them to go away. Take your puppy riding in the car when you go to grab fast food or head to the post office. If there are people working outside, bring puppy out so he can see and hear the activities. When the puppy has finished those vaccines, then start getting him out to areas where there are even more people. Enroll him in a puppy socializing class. Go to local parks. That puppy should have met at least 100 people by the time he is 16 weeks old, closer to 200 if you do those five new places and five new people a trip every week. What if you bring home an adult dog? Same goals: the more people met, the more positive experiences had, and the more developmentally appropriate situations the dog is place in, the better he will adjust. (Just shoving your dog into every situation and demanding he cope could create fears and anxieties which may translate to aggressions; therefore, a trainer who can help you gradually expose your dog to novel things in a way suited for your individual dog may be a necessity).

Make going out with puppy (or adult dog) a positive experience. Bring food and toys, have people feed and play with your puppy. Negative experiences are as detrimental as no experiences. If you want a companion you can take anywhere and everywhere, you MUST work to create confidence, trust and the ability to handle the world when the puppy is young. Even if you wish to adopt an adult dog, you must be willing to do the socialization work.

Mattie wanted a cute fuzz ball she could carry around in a purse or basket. She wanted a dog who could go with her everywhere and who would love visitors. However, Mattie failed to do any puppy socializing with Fizgig. When Mattie began to socialize Fizgig, she went about it by stressing her companion and forcing situations that the poor adolescent was unable to manage. If he showed stress and barked, Mattie punished him. Because he was shoved at people, punished for showing stress and then people were allowed to suddenly pick him up, Fizgig did not view people as good things. By the time Fizgig was presented to me, he was a fear-biter. Isolation and then improper socializing created a dog Mattie could not take anywhere.

From the moment that puppy (or dog) comes into your home, you are training, exposing and laying that foundation for what you need the dog to become. If Mattie did not work hard to rehabilitate Fizgig, what would the next 15 years be like? Yes, you can teach an old new tricks. It is easier to create the behaviors you want from the start than try to undo years of inappropriate work and the subsequent behaviors. Mattie owned the first dog in a class that had ever bitten me. (Mattie thrust Fizgig at me as I was sitting down, allowing him to observe me and accept I was no threat. Fizgig panicked as he landed near me and he gave a warning nip that did break skin). I worked privately with Mattie and Fizgig after that incident. Sadly, Mattie kept complaining that Fizgig was not rehabilitating. I could tell her why. I had seen her in the neighborhood doing exactly what she was being taught not to do. Not one lesson I gave was employed outside the sessions with me. No way could Fizgig be what was demanded of him if Mattie did not make the commitment to creating a true companion.

PROTECTION

The need to protect property or person is another reason why many consider getting a dog. However, dogs may not be the best protection and may become a liability. First, do you want a dog to alert bark or one who will actually take down a human? Any dog can be taught to alert bark. You do not need the biggest, strongest, most aggressive dog you can find in order to have a dog that will alert to a stranger and then quiet on cue. Getting a dog as a "man-stopper" is a whole other ball of wax.

Before you get a dog for protection, think long and hard. Many compare a dog for protection to owning a gun. This is a poor comparison. Guns are safer. Dogs are thinking creatures. A gun cannot think. Dogs are reactive to stimuli. A gun is not reactive. Dogs will react even if there is no owner present. A gun needs human manipulation to make it fire. No matter how well trained a dog is, at some point he may decide to react. A poorly trained and managed "protection" dog is a serious liability. That "watch dog" lying in your driveway may decide a child walking past poses a threat. Are you willing and able to do the socializing, training, provide a safe environment for your dog and the community? Are you willing and able to keep up with training and management of a protection dog? If you think you are, go spend time with a good protection dog club or trainer and learn. Talk to people serious about creating a well-trained and managed protection dog. Be as educated about this undertaking as possible long before you make that purchase.

So you decide that a protection dog is just too much for you to consider. What about a dog to just alert bark? That same barking dog, if not properly managed, can quickly become the neighborhood nuisance. You could end up finding yourself with noise complaints filed because your dog barks at everything, all the time and your neighbors refuse to tolerate the situation. A dog still needs training to bark when there is a reason (someone on the property) and silence on cue or when the threat has passed. Are you willing to do this work? Yes some breeds were developed for a stronger protective drive, but this does not absolve you of proper socializing, training and managing the dog. If the only reason you want a dog is for home protection, you would be wiser to install a good alarm system and a battery backup. "Why?" you may ask. Statistics show dogs are great for deterring crime and you can get one cheaply from the pound. Alarm systems require installation and the initial cost may be more than a dog. Heck, you can get a dog for free! Let's look closer:

An alarm system does not require food, exercise, training or veterinary care and can save you insurance money. A dog needs daily food, exercise, training, veterinary care and can be a liability causing you to have to pay more for insurance premiums or even lose your insurance if your policy has restrictions based on breed or training. What will happen when the dog gets older and cannot perform the duties as effectively? Many larger breed dogs are seniors by the time they are seven to nine years old. A dog at age eleven may not be anywhere near as effective a "watch dog" as the same dog was at age four. However, the dog may still have several more years on this planet. What will you do with that senior dog? An alarm system, if properly installed and maintained, can last for many more years than a dog.

I did an evaluation for a single mother, Mrs. Lennon, who purchased a German Shepherd pup because Mrs. Lennon felt she needed home protection especially for when her daughter, age 12, was home with the baby sitter. She was talked into getting a dog for protection by a friend who was, guess what, a German Shepherd breeder, who just happened to have puppies to place. She acquired Lizette. Mrs. Lennon was also convinced that in order to create a protective dog, she had to isolate Lizette from all human contact except for her, her daughter and a select few friends.

Lizette was only walked after dark and kept chained behind a barrier so she could not see anything. To make matters scarier, the primary trainer/caregiver was the young daughter. This pup may grow up thinking every human is a threat that must be engaged. Isolation will do nothing but create a dog with fears and quite possibly fear-related aggressions. By the time the pup is a year old, the child will be unable to safely control the dog. Should Lizette decide that everyone is a threat, what could happen? The only reason Mrs. Lennon called me was her vet insisted a trainer be contacted as the puppy was exhibiting worrisome behaviors at just a few months old.

I knew people who did Schutzhund and Protection work, I knew the level of socializing and training needed to create an effective and safer animal. I carefully explained this to Mrs. Lennon. I offered to give her contacts for people who could help her create what she felt was needed but also create a safer companion at the same time. Mrs. Lennon said she will continue what she is doing as she believed in order to protect, the puppy needed to fear. I hope she has a good lawyer.

CHILD/CHILDREN ASKED FOR

This is a very popular reason people get dogs. As a parent and a former child, and one who works with families and dogs I can honestly state the average child will lose interest and the care will fall to the parents. I tell parents to get a pet for themselves and have the children help. No matter how much that child begs and promises, a dog is often too much responsibility and may be in the house longer than the child. If you get a dog when your child is ten and that dog lives until fifteen… I'll let you do the math. Are you willing to care for the dog even after your child has left the house? Go check out any online list and visit shelters and see how many pet are being/were given up when the child lost interest or moved out.

I have a houseful of pets. At the time of writing, we share the house with four dogs, six cats, two guinea pigs, a chinchilla, a gerbil and a bunny. My two children are not solely responsible for them. I am the main cage cleaner, feeder, brusher, poop-scooper and handler. My husband is right there with me with doing the work needed if I am out. My children assist and learn. If you are not ready for a 10 – 18 year commitment to a dog, no matter how much your child drives you insane, it is your responsibility to say "No!" It is better to upset a child than to sew that child up when that pup you really did not have the time for injures your child in play or defense. It is better to have your child "hate" you for a few days than the possible alternatives.

Mr. and Mrs. Smyth had three children under tem which mom home-schooled, a grandparent with some physical limitations living with them. After a lot of pestering, the parents gave in and got the children an early Christmas Puppy, Lolita. I was called when the pup was barely 12 weeks old. It soon became apparent that Mom was overwhelmed, Dad was not helping, Grandma kept doing things that encouraged the pup to jump and bite and then she would complain the pup was a pest. As for the children, well I have seen more peaceful riots. I was able to get the children to behave while I was there and interact in a safer manner with the pup. I was able to get the pup to give me the behaviors the family needed. I was able to get Mom to reproduce the lessons very successfully with the pup and children. My written lesson supplements included how to integrate puppy work with the homeschooling curriculum. Physical education, science, hygiene/health, even writing, language arts and math lessons could all be done with the pup as a focal point. Math? YES! If we have Lolita sit four times and the down three times, how many behaviors has Lolita given us? Let's do this and see. Phys Ed and Agility! The potential I saw with this situation excited me! Sadly, Mom refused to work with the puppy or her children between sessions. She said over and over it was too much work. She would not allow herself to see that the work done now would prevent future issues. One session, I had my daughter come with one of my dogs. We met Lolita and her human, in a lovely little town. My daughter, six at the time, took the lead of that session. It was amazing. By the end of the session, Lolita was enjoying herself. Mrs. Smyth was relaxed and saw the improvements! She saw how well a young child could enhance training. Then she snapped "But I am not a dog trainer, my children are spirited and need to express themselves, so it will not happen."

Mom and Dad Smyth felt the children needed a dog to be fulfilled. I think it was more Mom hated to say "No" to her children and Dad who was rarely around when I was there (he was in his MAN CAVE), just did not care. While I was there Mom never did anything to stop undesired child behaviors nor did she even attempt to teach them proper behaviors. When I asked why she refused to teach the children safer behaviors and canine interactions, she would reply, "I do not like to crush their spirits and creativity." If the children were jumping on top of the crate while puppy was in there, Mom would not intervene. Then Mom wondered why the puppy was developing crate aggressions. Come on, it was becoming a box of torture! The children would pester, wear Mom down and do/get what they wanted. Eventually they focused on getting a dog and Mom gave in. No child NEEDS a dog.

Dogs are a great asset to the right home; however, in the wrong situation, a puppy could be a tragedy in the works. Already, Lolita had begun biting the children to get them to stop tormenting her. The children also taught the pup it was fine to tackle them and bite in play. The mother refused to give the puppy the physical and mental activity needed because it took away from homeschooling. By now, the pup, if still in the home, outweighs all three children. A simple "No, we are not getting a dog" then sticking to it, would have been a better decision.

Another option is short term care of a dog or puppy. If your child loves dogs but you do not want the long-term commitment, consider fostering a dog for a rescue or raising a Service Dog pup. The commitment time will vary and you will receive a serious education for your child in regards to responsible dog husbandry. There are many things your family can do that involve working with dogs without the long-term commitment of actual ownership.

RECOMMENDED BY ANOTHER

What works for me may not fit your needs. Suggesting someone look into breeds is one thing but then it is YOUR responsibility to ensure the suggestion is the best match. Do not go blindly by recommendation alone. Say you want a dog that is good with children and your neighbor recommends a Labrador. Hey, you have seen them on TV and they are always great with kids, on TV shows. You have no idea that Labs can be quite active, shed and have a tail capable of clearing a coffee table. You end up miserable because you are not an active person, hate dog hair all over the place and have a house full of low shelves and tables covered in antiques. A Lab may be perfect for your neighbor, but the worst choice for you.

One of the scariest calls I ever received came from a parent of a child with serious, aggressive, behavioral disorders, excessive hyperactivity, and mental delays. His pediatrician recommended that Mom obtain a German Shepherd in order to keep the child in line and well exercised. Mom was unsure of this recommendation and decided to seek canine professional advice. I was glad she decided to make a few phone calls before running out to the first person with a litter or the local pet shop. I spent over an hour on the phone discussing various concerns. Mom realized that this was not a good recommendation and even mentioned finding a different doctor.

A local radio garden guy used to suggest getting a small terrier to help control varmints in the garden. I sometimes got calls from people wanting terriers for rodent issues, but had no idea about any of the other commitment issues.

Dogs can be therapeutic and helpful in the right situation. Look at therapy dogs and service dogs, dogs working to rid farms of vermin or protect livestock. Then realize these success stories were carefully thought out situations. If you get a dog solely because another suggests a dog will fix X, it can end disastrously

Dogs are not medication, rodent traps or anything else alone. Dogs are living creatures with physical, social and behavioral needs.

Alice and Amy were mother and daughter. They had a small farm and needed a

dog to help guard their goats and chicken from coyotes. Yes, even in the Washington, DC suburbs, we have coyotes. The man they spoke to at the local feed store said a Border Collie would be a great farm dog. Alice and Amy needed a livestock guarding dog and neglected to tell the feed store owner what they needed for abilities. Border Collies are herding dogs. A herd is a modification of a hunt. Alice called me trying to figure out why the dog kept chasing the goats and chickens as opposed to protecting them from harm. The job at hand was not suited for a Border Collie. The job they had to fill needed a livestock guarding dog like a Great Pyrenees or Kuvas. Luckily, I was able to get them started in basic manners and eventually into Agility classes. The dog would never be what they needed for the job, but she could still be a good dog with a more suitable job. I also steered them towards people who would help Alice and Amy get their livestock properly protected. Had Alice done a little homework and had Alice had meaningful, prior dog understanding, she would never have put her livestock at risk. Alice had no farm experience either; she just thought a small farm would be a good thing for her daughter.

WORKING PARTNER

Most people that fall into this category have already decided they want a dog and are just trying to find the best match. Some are hunters or want to participate in a canine-related activity such as Agility and are getting ideas for what may suit their needs the best. Others have disabilities and are considering having a dog privately trained as opposed waiting for one to come from an organization.

However, you must remember that not all dogs will make the grade for what you need. I have known Labs that would not retrieve or swim though this is what the breed was developed to do. It is important that if you are looking for any working companion to not only choose the dog carefully but the source. Look for someone breeding or volunteering with a breed-specific rescue who knows how to screen for potential working ability. It is also important that you choose the right dog for the job. A Komondor is not a good choice for someone who wants to do Earth Dog work. A Beagle is not a Livestock Guarding Dog. A Chihuahua is not suited to be a Service Dog if the human needs light switches turned on and doors pulled open.

A woman I trained with years ago was interested in Search and Rescue work. She had the time, the money and the dedication. She had done her research and knew this was her calling now that her children were grown. Over time, she joined a superb organization, learned about the dogs, what would be needed, etc. After careful research into breeds that would not only suit her home life but also the job at hand when duty called, she acquired a lovely White German Shepherd Dog. Last I knew the two were preparing for their final test before officially becoming an S&R team.

VANITY

Sadly, many owners get dogs to be little more than accessories. This is part of the reason why there are issues with certain breeds or types of dog. Too many greedy humans are more than happy to fill your desire to be whatever image you dream with haphazardly bred dogs. The trendier a dog becomes, the harder it can be to find a good source. That cute boutique with puppies for sale alongside specialty handbags probably looks more appealing to the fashionable shop-o-holic than a well-chosen rescue or breeder. What better to complete your "gangsta" look like that musician on TV than a rugged, macho dog? Do not confuse the desire for a companion with vanity. Under no circumstances should a dog be purchased solely because you think the dog compliments or enhances your appearance. This is vanity. Companionship is the desire to share many years with a companion, through good and bad. Vanity is how will this make you look and will be changed with the next trend.

Little Annie will always have a special place in my heart. She should be called Number 5. Annie's owner was referred to me for help with Annie and her younger buddy, Cleo. Annie was an adolescent Yorkshire Terrier. Annie and Cleo lived with an elegant, single woman with a taste for the expensive and her equally vain mother. Yorkies were developed to hunt small vermin in the Yorkshire region of England. These little guys can be all terrier. Their owner wanted dogs like she saw in those lovely paintings: quietly posed on pillows, luxurious hair draped about, darling little bows, etc. This woman's home was elegant, museum-like, pristine, and a certain dog would just be the icing on the cake!

Now, why was Annie better named Number 5? The owner had gone through several dogs prior to Annie in her search for that perfect lounging pup to compliment her décor and fashion sense. The first dog turned out too big (Labrador Cross). The second dog was too active (West Highland White Terrier). The third and fourth dogs barked. Annie, a Yorkshire Terrier, was Dog Attempt #5 but now turning out to be too active and inquisitive; not a laid back dog at all. So the owner bought Cleo, also a Yorkie.

After a couple months of working with me, the owner decided that Annie had to go. Annie ended up a garage dog, filthy, bored and into mischief. Annie just wanted activity. She was bright, learned fast and loved being the center of social events. Instead, she was a garage dog. If the yard was fenced, she would probably be the outside dog. I found a breed rescue two states away that had a space for Annie. I was given the status to act as an agent for the rescue and presented Annie's owner with surrender forms. She signed the documents all too happily. Annie spent a few days in my home, getting cleaned up and having a chance to be a dog. The next weekend, my daughter and I drove over two hours to get Annie to those who would find her a forever home.

Cleo was not so lucky. Her owner would not relinquish her yet. I worked one *more session with Cleo after the owner moved to a new, million plus dollar home that better fit her image. One day, the child of a cleaning woman opened Cleo's crate, pulled the pup out and dropped her. Cleo ended up with two shattered front legs. The surgery was over $6,000 and the owner, just having returned from a European tour, had no money to cover the orthopedist. She called me to find her financial help. She owned a million dollar home, probably the same in décor, drove a $60,000 vehicle and had no money to save her dog. Six dogs bought in the name of vanity. Only one I know had a happy ending – in a different home.*

IMPULSE

You impulse buy a pair of shoes or a handbag, not a life. Often, these matches end up with a miserable dog and owner. No matter what your heart or even selfish impulsivity states, never buy a dog because you like what you see in the window. Dogs are a much longer commitment than a few days. Impulsive owners can make it work, but they have to be willing to devote the time and money.

Jordan and Jess saw a pup at an adoption fair. They were getting cat supplies and never had thought of a dog. Impulsively, they adopted the pup and the rescue group allowed people to take the dogs directly from the fair (much like shopping at a pet store). Luckily, the couple had dogs in the past and knew how to get started. I was called in to help keep them on track because it had been years since either had lived with a puppy. This was an impulsive decision that had a good ending. Later, they used me as a reference for a second, better thought-out adoption!

WHY DO I WANT A DOG?

Whatever your reason, you need to make sure your motives are in the best interest of the dog and not yourself. Dogs are not robots, alarm systems or rat traps; dogs are multifaceted creatures. Yes, dogs can and will, in the right home, excel at being any or all of what you want. However, you must look inside yourself and at your life. Can you give a dog what is needed to be happy and healthy within the scope of what you want a dog to do? Being chained up as a deterrent, toted around all day in a purse and replaced when no longer tiny and cute or shunned by adults who never really wanted the dog, is no life.

CHAPTER TWO

AM I READY FOR A DOG?

Once you have determined that your reasons for wanting to share your life with a dog are valid and in the best interest of your situation and fair to the dog, you must look at what you have to offer in order to help make that best match. I break readiness for a dog into the follow items you need to consider:

TIME COMMITMENT

Time commitment falls into two main categories: daily and long-term.

Many behavioral issues I work with have roots in a lack of **daily time** commitment. Some commonly acquired may need a couple hours of human led exercise and interaction a day (you walking and actively interacting with the dog) to meet their physical and behavioral needs. Bored dogs, ones with too much energy and not enough proper outlets are more likely to develop behaviors owners find annoying. The dog is not bad; he is just being a dog and trying to meet his own needs. The daily time commitment a dog requires will vary based on the type of dog and age.

All dogs need training and that training worked into daily life so they can learn house manners and rules. All dogs need some form of mental activity. Again, boredom leads to issues owners may not want such as chewing, digging, barking, chasing, and general destruction. Then the owner thinks the dog is being vindictive: no, you have a very bored dog trying to meet his needs.

All dogs need socialization so they do not develop fears or aggressions to the unknown. This socializing needs to be done daily in the beginning.

What about other things in the house that require commitment? Will you make the time to teach your children how to behave around a dog? Just training the dog is not enough. A child can undo all your hard work.

Are YOU willing to do the work or are you going to pass it on to a housekeeper, nanny or boarding kennel/boarding training staff? What will happen when that housekeeper or nanny gets fed up and leaves? Boarding-training does not absolve you of having to work with your dog and practice applying what the dog learned to your home. You can use dog walkers and such to SUPPLEMENT what you do, but it is not fair to expect someone to do all the work so you can relax.

Brad and Janet had a lot to offer a dog, just not Adam. Adam was large, active and very energetic. Five miles of walking a day was just a warm up. One day Adam was taken over ten miles in three walks and Adam was finally tired. Adam was also a thinking dog. Give that dog a challenge, a job and he would do it with flair! After keeping charts and tracking his physical and mental activities, it was determined Adam needed three to four hours a day, every day, minimum of physical and mental activity to meet his needs. This was not including integrating manners work into daily life. Adam was high maintenance to the extreme because of his physical and mental needs. Adam's owners were unable or unwilling to make the commitment to Adam. Even when alternatives and other resources to tap in order to help meet Adam's needs were presented, it was not done. No way could Adam's behaviors resolve when the poor pup was like a tempest in a teapot: too much energy and no release.

Over the months, Adam deteriorated and his owners were going crazy. Brad and Janet could not keep up with Adam. The few times Brad and Janet met his needs, Adam improved. Sadly, the couple decided they could not do this every single day for the next ten years. Adam was also a breed known to maintain these traits into late adulthood. His daily needs were great and the long term was frightening for the owners as they learned just how much of a commitment a dog like Adam was.

*****

Sally was a fun little girl, with a couple minor issues. She loved to chase the vacuum cleaner, bark at the hairdryer and had fears of walking past car tires. She came to her new home with these behaviors already in place. The rescue foster home had done nothing to work with Sally according to the couple, and told them to contact me to help resolve these behaviors. The woman in the house worked from home, part time. She spent much of her day watching TV. The husband worked out of the house but was willing to do all behavior modification exercises needed when he was home. I outlined and taught the couple simple exercises that could be done every day for a few minutes at a time that would help desensitize Sally. Within a couple sessions, Sally was significantly improved and just needed a bit more time to fully be the dog the couple wanted. Then it ended. The wife plainly stated that the desensitizing program would not happen and that she would not do the exercises to which Sally was rapidly responding. Sally was an easy dog: she just needed a little more daily work to fully come around. The wife would not even commit to a couple more weeks of work to finish what her husband and I had started. Sally was not like their first dog, who the wife missed. With half a chance, Sally could have been a wonderful companion.

*****

Mugsy lived in a mansion. His owners were far past "well-off" and they had a staff to care for the older teen children, private nurse for an ailing grandparent, staff to cook, clean, cater to whims. I was called because Mugsy (a puppy) was still having issues. Mugsy was bought as a companion for the wife. The nurse hired to give full time care to a seriously ailing, elderly family member, was expected to raise and train Mugsy in addition to her already extensive duties. The *wife was furious that Mugsy was not bonding with her, would not listen to her and he was no fun. She refused to do anything with the pup! She insisted her staff do it so she could enjoy their work. Guess who the pup bonded with? The staff was who Mugsy sought out for fun. The nurse was burning out and informed me she was looking for another position. The owner had the time to invest, she chose not to.*

Are you willing to commit to the dog's needs **for the dog's life**? This could be 10 - 18 years. This does not sound like a lot. Fifteen potato chips is not a lot, neither is fifteen chocolate chips. Fifteen years IS a lot. Let me break down what 15 years can be. The first dog I ever formally worked with came into my life just before I turned ten. She was with me for just shy of 16 years. This meant she saw me through the end of elementary school, middle school, high school, college, through marriage and purchase of our first house. My Ryker, now passed, saw me through two moves, the beginning of my business, and the birth of two children (five years apart). My D'Argo was the dog both my children learned the beginnings of Conformation Handling, grooming and Agility with. He is now almost 12 and retired. My son was about 18 months when we got D'Argo and my son is 13 at the time of publishing.

Long term means looking ahead and preparing for the future. How many dogs are given up when a family moves or adds a child? In most cases, surrendering the dog is done for convenience or the owners failed to prepare and will not try to make life work. (Alternatively, the couple cannot because the dog's behaviors are so out of control and the time to help resolve with an infant is not there). Most dog-baby issues I am called into work with are because the owners never prepared the dog for the baby. They never socialized the dog to children before a pregnancy occurred. No preparation work was done at all during the pregnancy. When the child was born, the dog's life was thrown into change, turmoil and he was expected to deal with it. How many people know months in advance of a job transfer yet wait until the last moment to look for housing? Now they cannot find housing that will allow them to bring the dog. The moment you know of a transfer, you need to investigate housing options so you are not stuck last minute.

Daily and long term commitment: are you able to do it? Are you willing to do it?

HUMAN MEDICAL ISSUES

Are there any allergies or medical conditions in your family that could cause issues resulting in having to get rid of the dog? *There is no such thing as a hypoallergenic dog regardless of what a breeder, rescuer or pet shop clerk will tell you.* People with serious allergy problems may not be able to tolerate ANY breed – regardless of what someone's ad or article indicates. Depending on the severity of the allergies or what part of the dog you are allergic to, no amount of cleaning, grooming or medication may give relief. What about other care needs for a family member? Are you the primary caregiver for a person with significant medical or behavioral needs? Can you also devote to the daily needs of the dog while caring for the human?

Earlier in this book I mentioned a woman who was advised by her child's pediatrician to get a German Shepherd to help keep her son in line and manage his behavioral issues. After an extensive discussion with the mother, I learned her son's issues were severe. At the same time, I was working with doctors to help diagnose my son's developmental concerns. I could empathize. With the amount of time her son required and the severity of the issues (including violence), she understood that getting any pet was a bad idea. Her son needed too much devotion and a dog would end up suffering, possibly getting hurt or even hurting her son.

*****

Amelia was a mother of three children, two in preschool and one at home. One child and her husband both had severe allergies to dogs. They fell for the "This cross is hypoallergenic and they do not shed." Within a week, the two who were allergic to dogs were miserable and the puppy returned to the breeder. I did let the mother know that there is no such thing as a hypoallergenic purebred or crossbred dog. She had no idea and fell for a common canine myth. There have been various studies on allergies to dogs I recommended she read. Again, there are no hypoallergenic dog breeds or crosses.

Along with medical issues, you must address physical abilities due to age, accident, birth, etc. This is a very touchy subject but is one you must consider before acquiring a pet.

Can you physically manage the dog you want at this stage in your life? What about five to fifteen years down the road? What provisions will you make should your dog outlive you?

One of my clients was a very sweet and loving woman of a respectful age. She had a lot to offer a dog; however, she made the wrong choice and the rescue group she worked with was reckless with helping her choose a dog. She said she had owned German Shepherds before, yet she was forty years younger at the time. A rescue coordinator placed a young adolescent German Shepherd in her home. The Shepherd placed with her was already familiar to me as the rescue director had tried to get the woman fostering her to work with me regarding behavioral issues they were seeing in the entire litter of purebred German Shepherd puppies surrendered to the group. The foster care giver for this pup failed to address the issues and by now the dog was a mess. I had advised no placing of her until she was rehabilitated and the director did not listen. By the time this pup was placed, she had developed serious anxieties, was large, still growing, active and STRONG. The foster care giver then placed the dog in a home that the director had serious reservations about regarding the ability to meet dog's needs and potential adopter's physical abilities. The potential adopter did not want to admit that with her current abilities, this dog was not a wise choice. The saddest thing was the rescue had many smaller dogs, adult dogs with training, which would have been a far better match.

*****

Another potential client was on oxygen, could barely walk more than a block and had other medical issues. He chose a young husky mix. The dog was developing serious issues based on the owner's lack of ability to give the dog enough outlets for his energy levels. The dog was becoming destructive, escaping constantly, had become the neighborhood menace and on the verge of doing something serious. When the owner was younger, he had big, active dogs; however, now that his health was not what it was, he chose what he knew best but would not admit he could not give the dog what was needed.

In both cases, the owners could care for a dog and did have family who would step up in the event that the owners could no longer care for the dog. Neither owner was in any physical condition to handle the dogs they chose. Both over estimated their physical abilities. The owners chose poor matches. Before getting a dog, you must determine if there are any medical or physical issues with you or a family member that will affect your ability to care for the dog you desire. Now, I have worked with clients who were disabled and did wonderfully with their dogs. They chose breeds that they know they could meet the needs of and worked diligently from the time the pups were young to cultivate the behaviors and manners needed. It can work!

COST

Can you afford a dog? Getting the puppy or dog is not the big expense: free to a couple thousand dollars. What follows can drain your wallet. Buying the crate and other necessary supplies, puppy inoculations every few weeks while the puppy is young; training classes; annual wellness checks; feeding a good food; medical emergencies, etc., that will drain the bank account. I spent $100 to adopt a dog but hundreds to get what I needed for supplies for a dog much larger than I had gear for, have him neutered, enroll in classes for socializing, vaccines as his records had been lost by the surrendering owner, etc. This was in 1996. Many dogs are given up due to costs. When the economy goes down the drain, jobs are lost, people retire, etc., it may be a pet that is the first expense cut.

I break down costs into several categories: initial, ongoing, unanticipated. Before I continue, please remember there is NO such thing as a free dog. You may be given a dog but you will still have other expenses. Now, you may continue.

INITIAL

       Cost of the dog
       Crate
       Leash and collar
       Vet check after adoption/purchase (do within 24 – 48 hours)
       Licensing
       Microchip / identification
       Toys
       Grooming supplies
       Socializing and training classes
       Spaying or neutering
       Bedding

ONGOING

       Food
       Heartworm preventative
       Treats
       Replacement toys and supplies
       Veterinary visits/vaccinations (as a pet ages, you may find yourself with increased visits)
       Licensing
       Professional grooming if needed
       Boarding for vacations

UNANTICIPATED

       Emergencies
       Medication for a chronic issue
       Supplies/environmental changes needed
       Additional training/behavioral work
       Increase in insurance costs
       Dog walker/day care

Because costs change, will vary based on the size of your dog, coat type, etc., these are all approximates of what in the average year I spend.

Food for all four dogs (kibble and canned)

       $45 a bag of higher quality kibble and I go through one bag a month
       $1.15 a can for higher quality canned and the dogs split one can a day

General medical care (annual checks, heartworm, flea/tick)

       $150 - $300 / dog for annual checks depending on what needs to be done

   $340 for all dogs for heartworm preventative
   $300 for all dogs for flea preventative

Grooming for my senior dog who does better with professional jobs now

   $300 / year

Now, I do take my dogs to classes every so often and cost averages $110 for six weeks. Even though I do not compete like I used to, my dogs still enjoy the work and it is beneficial.

Toys, chews, shampoos, replacing worn out supplies, etc…

Then there are those other expenses that are not annual but have to be considered when they do arise:

Medical emergencies, well I can easily drop $1,000 and then there are surgeries needed like removing a bothersome lipoma, a keratectomy when my big girl lacerated her cornea, etc., these can run a couple thousand dollars per incident. These are all expenses I have dealt with over the years.

However, there are ways you can save costs. Bulk buying food is one. Using vaccine clinics that many communities hold is another while using the vet for annual exams (just keep copies of vaccine records to show your vet). It is often cheaper to order toys and treats on line (even including shipping) if you shop around. Ask if your vet offers multi-pet discounts.

Jackson was a goon of a Lab. I swore he was deaf. He never seemed to hear anything nor did he respond to new noises. I conferred with his vet, we checked his hearing and his hearing was fine. There were also other behaviors I saw and physical issues that I was worried about. Again, more conferring with his vet and owner as medical issues can affect behavior. Finally, the vet determined that Jackson had some significant food sensitivities. Once the element he was sensitive to was determined by the vet and eliminated from his entire diet, Jackson was a new dog. His improvement was significant. Then he began to regress. The owner insisted she and the children were doing the work and keeping up with the new diet. So I poked around. Gone were the food and treats he was supposed to be on. Back were all the ones that Jackson had been eating at the start of my work with him. Jackson's owner could not afford the prescription diet and treats. I did some food brand investigating and found a commercial brand of kibble, cans and treats that were comparable to what he was on carried at a new local grocery. The ingredients Jackson was sensitive to were not in them! I bought her some of everything and Jackson turned around. I let Jackson's owner know where I found the food and encouraged her to head to the new store which was maybe fifteen minutes from her house. The food was a higher quality food and cost the same per bag as what she was feeding.

Dogs are a financial investment. The larger the dog: the greater the bills. The initial cost of a dog is nothing compared to what you will invest over your dog's life.

HOUSING

Can you properly house a dog? Being chained in the back yard with a hut and water is not proper housing for a dog you wish to be a companion. Dogs are social animals and should be part of the family unit. If you cannot make a dog a family member, keep him safely inside when you are not home and let him have plenty of exercise in a safely fenced area, reconsider. It is behaviorally devastating to a dog to be left outside all the time, alone, ignored, no work, etc. In addition, these dogs are more prone to becoming nuisance barkers, developing anxieties and ending up victims of "pranks" or theft. Electric fences fail, some dogs learn to tolerate the shock to escape the yard, and these fences can contribute to the development of aggressions over time because of the pain inflicted when the dog decides to do something ("I want to go greet person, I get hurt. People cause me pain. I have to get rid of people near my yard. I go to potty on grass, I get zapped. I potty inside, no zap.")

One potential client of mine called many times regarding a dangerous dog situation. Her yard was unfenced and the dog was left tied out all day when no one was home. Frequently the dog escaped, had bitten several adults on one of her escapades, and attacked a neighbor's child when the child toddled onto the unfenced property. Sadly, the owner did not want to invest any money into a fence or even a kennel and training. All I could ask her was if she knew a good lawyer. One of these days she will lose her insurance, be sued, animal control confiscate her dog or she may even lose her house because she rented and the landlord could be at risk for allowing the dog on the premises.

*****

Another client refused to realize that one dog was testing the limits and even crossing the electric fence line. The dog had been deemed dangerous by her county because the dog left the property and mauled a passing dog, the attacked dog was leashed. The county would not consider lifting the designation because the owner refused to confine her dogs in a safer manner. She spent thousands of dollars fighting the designation in court: more than fencing part of her yard would cost.

*****

Yet another client had to move because her dogs were all deemed risky by her former county authorities because she refused to install a better fence. She was given two options: leave the county (or at least the dogs had to go) or the dogs would be confiscated. She moved to a more rural area.

At her new home, one dog was permitted to leave the yard (unfenced and he was allowed on the front porch, nothing to confine or restrain him. He killed a cat that was on a neighbor's porch and bit the neighbor as he was trying to protect his pet. This dog had proven over and over to be the "street problem." The dog was reported to the authorities. The owner's options were: call in a trainer and fix the issues or the county would remove all her dogs. She still refused to do the environmental work to ensure her dogs were not a danger. She even began letting her dogs run off lead in the private fields near her house (without permission from the farmer who owned the land) and would bike with her off lead dogs running alongside. I stopped consulting on her case because the owner repeatedly refused to comply with local laws or consider public safety. She found another trainer who told her what she was doing was great for her dogs. I wonder if the trainer knew the history.

*****

Anna and Hanna were littermates adopted into a lovely and experienced dog home. However, the owners neglected to learn the fence requirements in their community. Anna and Hannah were large dogs. The owners contained them with a fence which was definitely inadequate for confining two large, active, athletic and curious dogs. The pups fast learned they could clear the fence with inches to spare. They became the neighborhood nuisances and a constant worry for the owners. Through adding a double fence, enriching the yard and increasing the human-led activity, we were able to stop the escapes and create a safer environment for dogs and community.

Are you willing to properly house and manage your dog? If you are not for whatever reason, your dog could become the neighborhood problem. In many rural areas there are laws stating if your dog is found in a field with livestock, the farmer may shoot your dog to protect his stock. What the dogs need to be doing may vary community to community and range from just being in the field to being in the act of chasing.

The Lewis family had two large dogs. The family moved to a rural area and felt it was fine for their dogs to have full run of the region. There was no confinement. Since the dogs always came back and were loving members of the family, the Lewis family was shocked to have a visit from Animal Control. The dogs had been witnessed chasing livestock at a neighboring property. The farmer was nice and was calling Animal Control instead of shooting the dogs. However, Animal Control let the owners know that if a responding officer saw the dogs in the act of physically mauling the animals, the law in the area was the dogs would be shot. The Lewis family ignored the warnings time and time again. The chasings became attacks. During one response, Animal Control found one dog ripping a ewe to shreds, a couple seriously injured sheep and the other dog sitting off to the side and he had bloody paws. The dog in the act of attacking the ewe was shot. The injured sheep were too far gone to save. The dog not seen actively attacking the sheep was returned to the owners, along with the body of the other. This is a story from my childhood. I knew several animal control officers in rural areas. This was told to me by an officer: the officer who had warned the Lewis family and later had to shoot the dog. I know a rancher who has had to kill loose family dogs she has found running her sheep. Her livestock guarding dogs have also killed loose dogs that jumped the fences and entered her pastures.

LIFESTYLE

What is your lifestyle like? Are you an active family that spends time hiking and camping or going for long walks? Are you more sedentary? Some breeds require a lot of exercise daily – both physical and mental. The half hour walk given to a Bulldog (often called an English Bulldog) is far from adequate for the average Border Collie. A Bulldog will not be able to handle the sometimes hours of daily workouts on which many a Border Collie thrives. Do you have frequent visitors that like to walk in unannounced? Some breeds may not adapt well to guests just strolling in the front door without your "approval." Research any breed thoroughly. Educate yourself carefully before committing. Use several different sources as well. What one person, a vet or trainer says about a breed may be erroneous. Look at books devoted to the breed; many breed-specific dog clubs have websites with plenty of information, contact rescues specializing in the breed you are considering. Many undesired behaviors start with the wrong match for the human's lifestyle.

If you are looking at a cross, research the breeds suspected in the cross to give you an idea of what you are getting.

Bear in mind that small does not equal less energy. Some giant breeds have lower activity levels than many smaller breeds.

Amy and Andy lived in the suburbs. They, especially Andy, were very active. After extensive research, they chose to get a German Shorthaired Pointer they named Sassy. Andy, Amy and Sassy ran every day. Andy ran before work and Amy, and accountant, worked from the house so she took her runs during the day. At night, they took long walks. Later, Andy became involved in field trials so Sassy could do what her breed was bred for. Amy knew that a dog was best in the house so she insisted on Sassy being taught solid house manners. By the time we were done, Amy had a dog she loved having in the house and Andy had the best behaved dog when he went trialing. Though many "dog people" cringe when they heard a GSP was living in the suburbs, Amy and Andy knew their active lifestyle and what they were interested in. They chose carefully and wisely.

GROOMING

All dogs need grooming – even hairless breeds have skin care needs. Some breeds are quite a bit for the average person to handle and may require professional work (Poodles and Bichon Frisés for example). Others require only a few minutes of going over with a brush once a week. All dogs lose fur to some extent. Even "no shed" breeds will lose hair. Hair falls out of follicles – look at your own brush or how often do you pluck a strand off your jacket. Humans are technically no-shed. Some breeds do shed less than others.

If you are a neat freak and cannot stand dust bunnies, consider a lower shedding breed. Then again, if you are a serious neat freak, a dog may not be a suitable pet. Coat length does not mean a breed will shed more or less. A short-coated breed can shed just as much as a medium to long coated one. Dogs with what is called a "double coat" will lose that insulating undercoat a couple times a year. In addition to brushing the coat (or tending to skin needs in the hairless breeds), you will have to trim nails, clean ears, clean teeth, etc. Certain medical conditions may increase or alter what you have to do for grooming or even address dietary issues. The amount of grooming you need to do, or have someone do, will be determined by the dog you choose.

Molly was a designer mutt often touted as being no shed, hypoallergenic and the perfect family pet (Goldendoodle). Louisa decided she needed a dog to complement her perfect family. However, she hated dust and hair. The cross Molly was included a breed KNOWN for shedding. This puppy was SHEDDING and Louisa was furious.

EXPERIENCE

Are you an experienced dog owner or is this your first one? There are many breeds not appropriate for a novice for one reason or another. Many people see dogs on TV, in the movies or music videos and must have one just like it. Obviously, these dogs must be great if they are in Hollywood! WRONG! What makes dogs excel in acting, Agility and other activities often makes them more (sometimes FAR more) than the average dog owner is prepared to handle. For example, thousands of Dalmatians, Border Collies, Rough Collies and Parson's (Jack) Russell Terriers found themselves given up by owners who HAD to get one because of the image Hollywood gave them. Some breeds can be a challenge to work with if you are not properly prepared to gain control *in a humane manner*. No breed has to be trained using harsh methods; however, there are breeds that are not good choices for owners with little to no dog experience.

No breed is stupid or less intelligent, regardless of what some surveys would have you think. You need to look at what the dog was developed to do when determining how good a match for your experience he may be. Expecting a

Bloodhound round up sheep as your neighbor's Shetland Sheepdog does when he competes in herding trials is ridiculous. I would not expect my Shelties to trail a fugitive or seek a lost child as effectively as a Bloodhound does. Hollywood or someone's suggestion should never be the litmus test of the appropriateness of a dog for your experience level. You need to get out and find people knowledgeable in the breeds you are considering and see if your experience level is suitable or not.

Boris, oh dear, Boris... Boris was a rare breed, high drive, massive even as a 12 week old puppy, his owners had no dog experience at all. Boris was a breed that you NEEDED solid dog experience to own. Had the people owned similar breeds successfully in the past, they would have been in a better position with Boris. The humans were all about the status and impression. Their friends all had more common breeds that would have been a better choice. This was not good enough – these people were trend-setters! After searching, they found a breeder willing to sell a pup. (Note: the rest of the breeders in the country they contacted refused the sale because of no dog experience). The owners were overwhelmed. Luckily I HAD worked with this breed before and was able to get them to make the needed changes. This could have turned out far worse.

YOUR FUTURE

What will happen to the dog if you start a family? Are you just going to dump the dog or do what it takes to ensure he is ready for the new arrival? Thousands of pets are given up because of a new child. Adding a child means more work and often less time for the dog. If you are military or travel extensively for work and may face reassignment, will you be able to take your dog? I have had multiple clients end up facing just this when they had a military or job move and were not able to bring their dogs. I currently live in a high military area; this issue is a big concern with local rescues. On the other paw, I have had many military clients who have very successfully moved dogs all over the country and the world.

Tilly was an awesome little girl. The couple was dog-savvy and had her enrolled in classes within weeks after adoption. However, the husband was active military and this was just after the September 11, 2001 attacks. The husband received deployment orders the week classes began. They made two classes and then dropped out. I got a phone call shortly after. The wife decided that she could not stay state-side without her man and where they were going, bringing the dog was not an option. Before adopting Tilly, they knew the husband would be deployed at any moment. However, they did not discuss what would happen to a pet when deployment happened. Tilly was given up.

*****

Ashton was a goof. He was picked up on the side of the road by a young couple. No owner stepped forward so his rescuers kept him. Ashton was very active and luckily the wife was a long distance runner and her husband loved long walks. When the wife became pregnant, they immediately began preparing Ashton for the new baby. The couple did not wait until the wife was scant weeks from birth to prepare the dog. Forethought and preparation helped make the transition from two and a dog to "and baby makes four" significantly smoother.

*****

The Colonel (as he liked to be called) and his family travelled all over the world due to his position in the military. They made sure that their dogs were all impeccably trained, could handle any change and worked hard to ensure with that every transfer, the dogs would be able to come. It was difficult at times, yet they committed to their dogs and did everything to keep their home a forever home - even if it meant sometimes the wife stayed behind with the dogs.

GOLDEN YEARS

What will you do as the dog ages? Are you prepared to cope with the onset of old age or when the dog is no longer "useful"? Can you handle the increased health issues that can go along with a senior dog? Will you be able to afford the extra expenses a senior dog can bring? Will you be willing to say goodbye when the time comes and not make your dog suffer needlessly because you do not want to cry nor will you dump the dog on a vet or shelter so you do not have to face the pain? A dog will spend his life trying to please an owner. The least we can do is make their Golden years truly golden and his final days pain-free.

Blizzard was a cool dog. A big, white Samoyed boy! His story was not as cool as his name. Blizzard was dumped at a local Shelter because he was old according to his surrender notes. He could not keep up with the family; he needed senior exams which cost more. Blizzard was just an old dog. Saddest was he spent most of his younger days tethered to a tree because he was big. Blizzard was not an adoption candidate: senior dogs are often considered unadoptable solely because people do not want old dogs. Luckily, he was so sweet that the shelter staff gave Blizzard a solid chance. He ended up with a young couple who knew that though he only had a few years left, that Blizzard was a good dog. At age 9, he found a new life. When Blizzard was ten, I was called to help prepare him for a new baby. Later, I ran into the family while I was working with another client in the neighborhood. Blizzard, now 11, was happily tottering along next to the stroller. Even as an old dog, Blizzard took to training and loved to learn.

AGREEMENT

Is the family in agreement as to what type of dog or even if a dog will be the pet? If the adult members of the house cannot agree, then it is a recipe for disaster. If one partner really dislikes the dog for whatever reason, this will affect how they interact with the dog. A dog that is confused is more likely to develop behavioral issues. Some of these issues can be dangerous. I have had quite a few clients where one spouse refused to listen to the other's wishes. The lack of agreement put some owners in risky situations.

One graphic case of a family not agreeing on a dog was started by a husband who had to have a Rottweiler, which he named "Hugo." Mom hated the breed; she wanted a much smaller dog. Mom, who was at home, was full time caretaker for the dog while her husband worked up to 12 hours a day, not including commute and her teen sons were in school. Mom had made it known loud and clear that she did not want a Rottie. Yet, she never told the breeder. I was familiar with the breeder and knew if she had spoken up, the sale would never have happened. Mom did not speak up at the breeder's and told me so. When the pup came home, mom was inconsistent and even harsh in her managing of the babe. As the dog grew into himself, he started trying to take control. I swear he was working to bring order to the chaotic environment.

I found Hugo very willing to work with a confident, calm and not-harsh person. When he was presented with clear order to the chaos, Hugo was a different dog. However, on more than one occasion, he had pinned the wife when she started to hit him or throw a prong collar around his neck to "force him" to behave. I told Mom that if she would change her ways, Hugo could be a great dog. He was even responding better to her during my time there, but then regressed. Mom refused to do the work as she HATED this breed. She would continue to do what she was and maybe someone would figure it out (she assumed Rottweilers were dangerous) and the dog would go. What Mom was doing was creating a dangerous situation that would most likely end up with a severely bitten lady and a dead dog.

LEGAL/MISCELLANEOUS

Are you able to own the kind of dog you want or the number of dogs? Many people assume they can have any dog they want or may be oblivious to pet number restrictions. Many communities are passing various restrictions and even outright bans on certain types of dog. It is erroneous to assume all rescues and breeders know where these restrictions are. Therefore, it is up to you, as a potential owner, to know if you can own what you want or not. In addition, you need to look at leases and home owners associations /covenant communities and insurance issues. Is there anything in your lease, HOA (home owners association) / covenant or insurance that could affect owning and managing a dog? It is easy to say you would be willing to move when something challenges your ability to own a dog. However, when push comes to shove, are you truly able to find a new home and potentially a new job?

Thor, HUGE dog, recent rescue from a neighboring state, underweight and still over 150lbs. Melanie owned this breed before and was a good match for Thor. She learned of Thor through a rescue website. Jumping at the change to once again own a breed she loved and rescue a dog, Melanie raced to the shelter. However, she forgot one thing: her HOA rules. She lived in a community comprised of closely spaced, stand-alone homes, condominiums/apartments and townhomes. The dog rules were clearly spelled out. Melanie knew the covenant and that in her section of the community, there was a weight limit. Thor exceeded that limit by over 100lbs, even in his current underweight condition. She never applied for a waiver as the HOA rules allowed; she just snuck Thor in, and admitted it to me. Her neighbors were already complaining. Melanie was risking the HOA demanding she get rid of Thor. To complicate matters, Thor had significant behavioral issues; severe fear aggression. His size and behavior made him a poor candidate for placement at that point. If he returned to the rescue, euthanasia was almost a guarantee. If he was placed at this point in a new home, his fears and the stress of yet another change could trigger a serious reaction. I applauded Melanie for rescuing a dog but her willingness to ignore HOA rules may end up with Thor paying a serious price.

What about number of pets? Some communities have limits on the overall number of pet you may have. They do not care if they are inside only or go in and out. If there is a four pet limit where you are and you have four cats, then bring in a dog, you are now in violation of the pet limit rules.

AM I READY FOR A DOG?

Time Commitment
Human Medical Issues
Cost
Housing
Lifestyle
Grooming
Experience
Your Future
Golden Years
Agreement
Legal/Miscellaneous

As you can see, many things must be considered before a dog arrives in the home. The vast majority of calls I receive are based in owner lack of preparation and thought which resulted in issues with the dog. Many times the issues are due to an owner not fully thinking through what a dog entails or having the ability to provide for said dog behaviorally, environmentally or financially. Before you even begin looking at the best match for you, ask yourself "Can I be a good match for a dog?"

CHAPTER THREE

WHAT TYPE OF DOG IS BEST FOR ME?

This chapter is broken down into several sections. These sections represent the majority of cases I have worked with regarding the choice of a dog and issues that can arise. Many of my clients ended up getting dogs based solely on recommendation and never fully researched the needs of the dog. This can lead to major issues if the needs of the dog cannot be met. Other clients got dogs based on media trends, to "keep up with the Joneses," or to be different. Many ended up with far more than they were able to manage. This chapter is designed to help you learn to determine the best match for your home. There is no perfect dog. You choose the dog that closest fits your individual needs.

PUREBRED OR CROSSBRED

First, you need to decide if you want a purebred or crossbred. This is a personal choice.

With over 440 purebred dogs recognized by legitimate kennel clubs worldwide, countless "designer dogs / designer mutts" recognized by many less than ethical registries and countless of wonderful crossbred dogs in various rescues, what kind of dog should you consider? Purebred or crossbred, what is better? Take a random sampling of dog owners and you will get a variety of answers. Some will be intelligent while others based on assumptions and rumor. Some people will be vehemently one way or the other, while some will say it is personal choice.

Purebred dogs have a standard that describes the ideal dog for the job it was bred to perform. This standard outlines size, colors, temperament, etc. Due to specific breeding for certain traits (size, temperament, color, work drive, etc), when one dog of a breed is bred to another dog of the same breed, you will only get dogs with those traits. This is why when you breed Great Dane to a Great Dane you will not get Chihuahuas. With purebreds from good sources, you have better idea of what to expect in terms of size, color, temperament and health. Yes, genetics are funny and you can get dogs that are too big or too small, coloring out of standard, etc., in general, there is greater overall predictability with purebreds.

There are myths about purebreds. Possibly the most common one is that purebreds are unhealthy and have bad temperaments. This is not true. However, I need to qualify this: if you go to a reputable breeder who knows the health issues in the breed and breeds carefully so to reduce and even eliminate the chance of passing an issue on, you stand a better chance of getting a healthy dog. If you go to any Tom, Dick or Mary who breeds because they have a couple purebred dogs but have no knowledge of health or temperament in the breed or a pet shop; you have a greater chance of getting a dog with problems. The quality of the dog is based on the integrity of the breeder. A better breeder works to breed the best they can. Sometimes genetics will throw a curve ball. This is just the luck of genetics. Do not use this as an excuse not to get a purebred if this is what you want. Choose your source carefully and you will be rewarded. (This is to be discussed in greater depth later). Now, what about those designer dogs? Are they really what they are touted? Quick comment here: no serious breeder will breed crosses. Serious breeders are trying to improve and maintain a breed or line's integrity. They are not breeding for fun sounding crosses. How can you tell if a dog is a purebred or a designer mutt? Look at registries:

In the United States, we have two main registries: The American Kennel Club and the United Kennel Club. If a breed is not recognized by them, then be suspect. However, neither registry recognizes all breeds: therefore, look at the Canadian Kennel Club and the Fédération Cynologique Internationale (http://www.fci.be) or the major registry reported in the country of origin. If the breed cannot be found in these registries, then it may not be a true breed. Some people have even created their own registries to give false credibility to designer dogs. This is deception. Another clue is does the name end in –oodle, -uggle, or any other cutesy thing or is the breeder trying to "recreate" a long lost breed or develop his own. With over 440 breeds in the world and the ability to import, there is really no need to do this. However, there are still people who intentionally or negligently create crosses. With so many crosses at shelters, there is no need to purchase from someone breeding them just to make money.

Crossbred dogs are wonderful. However, with crosses, you often have less to go by when determining the outcome, especially if you are getting a puppy or adolescent. My old Hunter was half Australian Shepherd and half Newfoundland. When I adopted him as an assumed younger adolescent, Hunter was already far larger than the average Aussie – but smaller than the average Newf. We would not know just how big he could get for another year or so. He was almost done with upward growth, but bulking out can go for some time with many dogs. Even as an older adolescent dog, final size was not fully determinable. Luckily, Hunter topped out in the upper seventies for weight and 23 inches at the shoulder for height! As for temperament: another guess.

Newfoundlands and Australian Shepherds are different in drives and energy needs. When Hunter matured, he could be bigger and goofy, larger-medium sized and goofy, high energy, more moderate with energy, etc. All we knew was he would be a larger dog, strong, potentially active dog and hairy.

When he grew up, Hunter took after the Aussie in temperament. Even as a senior dog, Hunter had more energy and drive than the average family is willing to endure. Up until he hit 11 years or so, Hunter was more than many people could deal with. He also had medical issues. Yes, a cross. You may ask about hybrid vigor as has been touted by many people over the years. Domestic dogs are all the same species. In addition, there are MANY health issues common to most breeds of dog. When you breed a dog with a health issue to a dog without it, it is possible for the puppies to be, in theory, healthier than the affected parent is, but the pups may carry the issue. Therefore, the issue can be passed on if the offspring are bred. Hunter had hip dysplasia, an issue found in just about every breed of dog. Since most people breeding crosses do not do the extensive health screenings a good breeder of purebreds will, you will always have a chance of getting a cross with inherited problems. For more on the topic, the late geneticist Dr George Padgett researched hybrid vigor in dogs. His research into canine health and breeding has given valuable information to dog fanciers. If you are like me and a total nerd, I strongly suggest you look at his works. If you still believe in the myth of hybrid vigor because a breeder said it exists, you need to look up this man's work!

Every crossbred dog is unique and deserves a great home. I wholeheartedly support the adopting of them from rescues. When you adopt a dog – purebred or cross – you are saving two lives. First, you adopt a dog that was unwanted by an owner. Second, you have opened up a slot in that rescue for another unwanted dog to get a chance at a home. Just remember that, especially with puppies, there may be a lot of unknowns. Some of the BEST dogs I have ever worked with were carefully chosen crossbreds. That funny little mutt will always hold a special place in my heart as no two are ever alike.

If you are looking for a dog to compete with, both the American Kennel Club and the United Kennel Club have opened several sports to crossbred dogs. Therefore, your options now are wide open for a purebred or crossbred!

William was a big boy: far larger than his owners anticipated. I was working at the shelter he was adopted from. William was a Miniature Poodle / Great Dane cross. The people who surrendered his litter owed a female Dane and a male Mini Poodle. They assumed that since there was such a huge size difference that keeping them both intact was no risk. They witnessed the breeding. William's adopters were experienced owners and fell in love with this puppy. About six months later, they returned William. He grew too big. It was clearly noted on his card and adoption papers that one parent was a giant breed. They hoped he would stay smaller like a Mini Poodle. Well, the genetics for size in this boy were all over. William could have been anywhere from medium to huge.

*****

Sunny was a cross, his adopters had carefully researched the assumed breeds behind him and had a solid idea what to expect and what range of sizes and behaviors. They did their homework! Sunny was awesome. Sunny had come through basic manners and was now working on advanced. Since he learned so quickly, I began challenging him more and started introducing behaviors needed for Rally obedience. During this time, the American Kennel Club opened up Rally, Obedience and Agility to crossbreds! We have a lot of AKC events in our region. The teenage daughter was enjoying working with Sunny so much that she was determined to register and begin competing with him. I referred them to a program that would further their Rally training. Last I ran into them, Sunny was just exploding in a good way and the family had adopted another dog who was shaping up to be just as much of a joy as Sunny.

The choice of purebred or crossbred is personal. Make your decision based on good research and ignore the rumors and myths.

PUPPY OR ADULT

What is the best age dog to add into your home? Many people feel older dogs cannot be worked with as they are set in their ways. Yes, adult dogs may have developed some undesirable habits that need to be worked out, but adult dogs often are less work than puppies in other areas. Adult dogs may have had some prior training, especially if you are acquiring a retired show or working dog, may have had some house training, etc. Adult dogs have greater attention spans and more bladder control. There are also no surprises with an adult dog regarding size and coat, especially if you are adopting a crossbred dog. Unless the dog has been shaved, often what you see is what you get for size and coat type.

Most issues I deal with in regards to pups stem from a lack of time or solid commitment from the owner. Puppies may have to potty every couple of hours. If they are trained to potty inside or are forced to due to lack of time, housetraining may become harder depending on what is or is not done. Puppies chew, explore, get into things, etc. They need a lot of guidance at this stage. The first two or three years as the puppy goes through puppy hood, adolescence and finally enters young adulthood can be trying for owners. What you got temperamentally as a pup may be different from what the pup matures into. However, puppies are blank slates in many respects. You may have fewer undesired behaviors from former environments to work out with a pup than with an adult dog. A quick note on puppy age: no puppy should be placed before 8 weeks of age. Though a pup may be weaned by six weeks, there is a lot of growth and development that happens the weeks after. A good breeder or rescue will use this time to prepare puppies for new homes, work on socializing, etc.

I have brought both puppies and adult dogs into my house. Each has their pros and cons. Just remember, puppies are a lot of work and mature slower than the old tales of by a year old, pup is grown up. Adult dogs are less work in many respects, but if the previous owner did not do a great job with the dog at first, you may have some things to work out.

WHAT BREED IS BEST?

After you determine what you feel would be the best age for your situation, now it is time to determine breed or type of dog. So, what breed is best for you? There is no perfect breed regardless of what friends, dog owners, veterinarians, trainers, behaviorists, breeders, relatives or anyone will say. **The best dog for you is the one that closest fits your needs and whose needs you feel comfortable meeting.** For example, if you are looking for a dog you can hunt waterfowl with, a Border Collie or Maltese would not be a great choice. If you are looking for a dog to herd sheep or excel in Agility, a Dachshund or Bassett Hound is not a good idea. If you are looking for a dog that has lower energy needs and will be content with a short walk and some light play, a Pointer may not fit the bill. Do you love long hair? Why consider one of the hairless breeds? If you do not want to spend hours on grooming, a long coated dog may not be for you.

Many pick a dog based solely on looks and/or recommendation and nothing else. They forget to research the breed or assumed breeds crossed in the dog they are considering.

Do an internet search for breed clubs and purebred rescues. Peruse various sites and compare information. You need to look at the pros and cons of each breed. Also, visit dog shows and talk to breeders and exhibitors. Just remember, dog shows are stressing so do not expect someone preparing a dog or getting ready to enter the ring to have the time to talk. Politely ask when would be a good time to come back and talk or ask if you can call them later in the week.

A good dog club website should have not only the breed standard on it, but also give insight as to what a good representative of the breed should be in regards to health and temperament. Not all club sites are equal so check out several. Find books written by people involved in the breed. Not all dog books are created equal. Many books sold at pet supply stores may not be accurate. I have found some to be the same generic information with different covers, pictures and limited breed-specific information. Grab a few books on different breeds and look at the content. Is it all the same once you get past the breed description? If so, avoid the books.

Consider contacting trainers for advice. Many of the dogs we deal with are more common breeds or common crossbreds. Some may not have experience with rarer breeds. However, a good trainer will research many different breeds in case one shows up in a class. Breeds are not the same temperamentally and a good trainer will realize this. I have been lucky with finding mentors and even working with more than my share of rare breeds. Though many dogs do not fit my needs or desires, I know they may fit those of others. However, I know trainers who cringe when they hear of a Shetland Sheepdog in a home with children or who hate American Pit Bull Terriers. Others heavily push breeds that are large and energetic on everyone who calls because this is what they prefer. Just because the trainer is a Labrador fancier does not mean a Lab is the right dog for you. A good trainer will tell you the pros and cons of a breed and be able to help you find more resources for education. Listen and even write down the information, then compare it to other things you have learned.

Millie was a very rare breed, only a couple thousand in the United States. I had experience with similar, more common breeds (and owned a similar, more common breed) which was why the owner was referred to me. Millie was a poor representative of her breed in regards to temperament due to owner error. Millie was a wreck and the owner refused to see this. Years later, I would see a few more of this breed at a local dog show. I got to speaking with the owners and mentioned I had worked with one of this type of dog. They doubted it due to the rarity. Well, I gave enough information and the owners knew exactly who the owner was. They had even tried to work with her but were shut out. I was pleased to be able to meet good breed representatives with solid temperaments. I told the exhibitors that I knew not to base my impression of a breed on a single negative interaction with one dog in a home with an owner was blind to the issues she was creating. Sadly they said the women had worked with other trainers and these trainers were basing their impressions on the breed only on this one dog. It happens: we are humans with likes and dislikes. I hope that trainers will look objectively and understand that this one bad example of a breed is not indicative of the breed as a whole.

When you research breeds, make sure you include the history of the breed as well as current uses. The Standard Poodle was once (and sometimes still is) used in hunting. Many of these dogs retain a strong work drive and are not the fluffy-frou-frou dogs too many laugh about. Though the Bulldog (sometimes referred to as an English Bulldog) is far different from its ancestors, many retain some of the temperament traits of their ancestors. They look silly and goofy but can be self-confident and not "blindly" obedient. Dogs bred to work independently of humans are still highly intelligent and can be great problem solvers. However, dogs bred to work independently may not be the "Let me follow you everywhere and do your bidding, Master," type dogs many owners want. Quite a few breeds categorized as Toys or Non Sporting in the American Kennel Club have roots in hard working dogs. Dalmatians are some of the more challenging dogs for the average person. Though listed as Non Sporting, they have far more energy than many owners want to handle. This breed was developed to work with horses and follow riders on horseback or carriages for miles. Dalmatians are great dogs but the average person getting one, after Disney popularized them in animation and live action, had no idea the energy level of the average Dal. Many were given up.

When I was in corporate America, I worked with a man who complained one day that his dog was not able to take long walks with him or go jogging. The dog tired out fast and was breathing heavily. I asked him what he got: a Bulldog.

HOW HIGH IS HIGH ENERGY?

Often we will hear people talk about low, medium or high-energy dogs but not really expand upon this. One person's opinion of high energy may be far different from mine. When asking about energy and exercise requirements, ask for more specifics. Often potential owners get vague answers such as "A couple good walks a day." Well a good walk for you may be fifteen minutes where a good walk for the type of dog you are considering may be an hour or more.

Every year humans give up thousands of moderate to high-energy dogs for behaviors related to lack of exercise and stimulation (boredom). Dogs of all energy levels need some form of exercise **every day**. The best is human led. Human led exercise means **you** are the one initiating and leading the program: walking, playing, formal training, sports, etc. An adequate walk or play session is one where the dog is not looking for more action immediately afterwards. However, later in the day he may be raring to go again. If a dog is looking for more activity shortly after a session is complete, he probably needs his exercise levels adjusted. Energy needs will vary throughout the life of a dog: what was good for a younger pup will be different for the same dog at age five and again at age twelve.

Note, each dog is an individual and even within the same breed, needs vary dog to dog. Within a litter, you may get a big difference in activity levels. Though the breed standard claims X, dogs do not read the books. I have run into some very active French Bulldogs and a low energy Border Collie.

I define energy needs of dogs as the following:

> **Lower Energy Dogs** – less than an hour of exercise a day
>
> **Moderate/Medium Energy Dogs** – one to two hours of exercise a day
>
> **Medium-high/Higher Energy Dogs** – up to three hours of exercise a day
>
> **High Energy Dogs** – **minimum** of three hours of exercise a day

Just sticking Fido in the back yard for hours a day is not proper exercise. In fact, you could create more issues from nuisance barking and digging to fence running, escaping and even aggression. Proper exercise is a combination of activities that busy the body and mind as well as increases social skills.

Be honest with how much you can truly devote to the dog's potential needs. If in doubt, get out for a couple weeks and just do activities (walk, go to the gym, etc) for that amount of time a day and see if you can manage it. If you cannot do it yourself, can you commit to the dog you are considering? You may wish to consider an older adult as dogs may slow down as they mature.

Several clients of mine purchased Jack (Parson's) Russell Terriers. The JRT owners knew the dogs were higher energy but did not realize just how much the dogs needed. One owner assumed that half an hour, twice a day would be adequate because that was a good workout for her. This was barely a warm up for her dog. All the dogs were developing undesired behaviors. The dogs were labeled bad, vindictive and worse. The dogs were none of these. They were just higher energy dogs not getting enough exercise and training. The happiest and most laid back Jacks I have met are those in homes where they are actively working (on farms keeping down vermin) or living in homes with owners who are actively participating in various sports and training several times a week. Dogs with higher energy requirements with owners not able or willing to meet these needs are miserable.

Over the years, clients of mine with higher energy dogs have used dog parks, day cares, agility and other sports or carefully used treadmills to supplement what the owners could not fully do. The creativity some have used was unbelievable. However they knew the dogs had needs and they worked to meet those needs. Owners who failed to meet the dogs' needs often ended up with more problems.

AM I EXPERIENCED ENOUGH FOR THIS DOG?

Many owners get dogs that are "more" than they realize. This is part of why research is so vital. If a good breeder or rescue tells you that you are not ready for a certain type of dog, respect that. Sadly, too many people search until they find a breeder willing to sell them a dog or until one shows up in a pound. Many of the breeds often termed Rare, Molosser (Molossoid), Bully/Bull and Terrier, etc., require experienced owners. Even some more common breeds should have experienced owners. When an inexperienced dog owner gets a dog requiring experience, the potential for trouble is increased. I am not saying it cannot work out, I am just saying that if you have never owned a dog in your life, I would never dream of telling you to get a Fila Brasileiro or a Central Asian Shepherd. The average dog owner would find it difficult to live in sanity with either of these breeds. For a very brief period, I was getting a run of emails from people wanting Filas. They heard the dogs were awesome guarders and "natural" protectors. The Fila is a breed that must have an extremely dedicated and knowledgeable owner.

For quite some time, I saw a local increase in owners with breeds such as Presa and Dogo Canarios, American Bulldogs, Cane Corsi (plural of Corso), etc. All these are wonderful dogs for the right home. If you love the looks of these dogs but are not ready for one, consider a similar breed. Get that experience first. Volunteer with rescues that deal with related breeds. If this is not an option in your area, find a breed better suited. There are so many breeds to choose from you should be able to find a dog that suits your experience level. Yes, it is possible to make things work should you really have to have a dog that is a lot of dog, you just have to be willing to commit and seek out guidance before things go south.

The Sykes family loved dogs and after much consideration, decided to look at a rare breed: Spanish Water Dogs. This breed maintained a lot of its historical behaviors because it is not as common. However, the Sykes family had experience with similar, more common breeds. They were able to make the adaptations needed for a breed that was still very much a working dog. Had the Sykes family had no prior dog experience at all, I would not have recommended this breed.

CAN I PHYSICALLY MANAGE THE DOG I WANT?

I know this has been covered but must be addressed again. Physical abilities and our ability to handle dogs is a very touchy subject but one requiring addressing. Look at your physical abilities due to whatever reason, even age-related. As we age, our physical and mental abilities wane to various degrees.

One of my mentors, now in her late seventies, was involved with Irish Setter rescue. She knew the breed inside and out. She overestimated her abilities one day and did something in her heart she knew was risky: walking two foster dogs at once. In addition, she paid for it big time: both her kneecaps were broken when the dogs pulled her down. The dogs saw a squirrel.

*****

A client of mine had a physical disability and sometimes required crutches. Her choice of breed was well suited for her abilities, smaller and easier for her to handle. However, when they got loose due to her negligence, (leaving doors open and not having the dogs trained well), she was unable to catch them. When we addressed this issue, trained the dogs not to dash outdoors and I adapted the lessons to her physical needs, the situation improved greatly.

Can you keep up with the physical needs of the dog? Just because you had Vizslas in the past does not mean you can keep up with the intense physical needs of the breed now.

I received a call from a man who used to be a long distance runner. He was an experienced Vizsla owner and knew the physical needs of the breed. At some point, he had a serious injury and he was unable to run. When it came time for another dog, he got a Vizsla. The dog was developing behavioral issues. During our discussions, I learned that the dog was getting far less exercise than this type of dog generally needs. If this could not be addressed, there was only so much behavioral modification could do. The destructive behaviors sounded like a desire to get energy released. The owner loved the breed but was unable to give this type of dog what is needed physically. He would have been better off with a dog that better suited his abilities.

WHAT IS THE BEST DOG FOR CHILDREN?

Before I begin this section, I cannot emphasize enough the need for proper training of your children. No matter how great the dog is, no matter how patient and tolerant, a child's actions will influence how a dog behaves.

Shadow was a senior lab. He was tolerant with the two young boys in the house. However, Shadow had cancer. His treatments were making him feel sick. He was tired and just wanted a break. One day, the older boy, who had been allowed to play hitting games, started throwing wooden blocks at Shadow. Shadow got up and moved several times. The mother felt Shadow should tolerate the boys. Shadow was a dog and was a Lab and therefore, in Mom's mind, had to put up with the boys. After several rounds of trying to escape and mom failing to intervene, Shadow growled, gave an air snap and walked off. Shadow was put down the next day "for being a dangerous dog." Later, the family gave up their cat because it was easier than teaching the younger child not to drag the feline around by the tail. The cat got fed up one day and the nails came out. Cat gone because "she was dangerous." You tell me, who was the danger? I would not allow these boys at my house and finally lost touch with the mother when our children went to different schools.

I am a believer that regardless of breed or cross, you get out of a dog what you put into the dog. There are breeds often not recommended for children. Some breeds may have lower tolerance levels to things. You need to research carefully. Read breed descriptions from various websites. Read books. Speak to rescues, various breeders and trainers. When seeking a dog for a home in which children live or if you may have them in the future, or have relatives with children that visit, make sure you find someone who has properly socialized the puppy or dog to children. A dog who has never experienced children or who has had negative experiences is not a dog I would recommend in a home with children or where children frequent – regardless of how much you like the dog.

Remember this well: any dog can be provoked into biting. Some dogs can go their entire lives without even lifting a lip. Other dogs will nip at the slightest thing. **There is no such animal as a 100% safe or a "never biting" dog.** Some breeds absolutely vilified by the media may be very good with children **IF** the dog is from a serious person breeding for sound temperaments, socializing well and you do the work to create harmony with your child and dog. I have worked with breeds always recommended for homes with children but the individual dog was from a questionable source and the owners did nothing to work with the dog and children. A good American Staffordshire Terrier (not a haphazardly bred, generic pit from the guy off the Internet) in a good home may be a better dog with children than a Goldendoodle (designer crossbred often touted as the perfect dog by people selling them) in a home where the owners allow the children to treat the dog badly. Look at "Carl the Rottweiler" from those wonderful children's books. A good

Rottie from an excellent source and in the proper home is a tolerant, patient and devoted dog.

I have consulted on various bite cases with children. The majority of the bites I have consulted on are rooted in the child doing something to hurt the dog, make the dog feel threatened or playing inappropriately with the dog. In some situations, the dog had questionable to no experiences with children before entering the current home.

I remember working with a family and a sweet crossbred. The family was worried that the dog was going for the child "with no warning." I sat and observed the situation and asked the family to do what was normal for a few minutes. I quickly saw the problem. It was no wonder the dog was developing issues. The dog was in a position in which she was clearly not comfortable. The child hit her, ran about like a maniac, yelled at and tackled the poor dog. The parents walked off and never checked on the pair. The dog was giving a lot of body language indicating her discomfort with the situation well before she even showed signs she was getting set to nip. I stopped everything and explained what I had observed. The dog had a lot of tolerance, but it would not last if the parents did not get serious about working with their child. My plan was to teach the child dog safety, teach the parents safer management and how work with the dog to build up her tolerance level to children even greater than it already was. However, the parents were not dedicated or sure if they could do the work with the dog and child, and were discussing giving the dog back to the rescue. Though the dog was a good dog for a home with children; her situation was creating a greater bite risk.

Even the most tolerant dog will bite if pushed far enough. A poorly supervised and managed child can teach a dog that the only way to stop the child's behavior is with a nip. Once a dog learns biting is the only way to stop something... It can be difficult to return the dog's tolerance level in that situation. If you cannot or will not properly supervise and teach your children, do not get a dog. The results could be more tragic than just a quick nip.

Some breeds may be subtle in body language. This means that the owner has less to go on when "reading" the dog. I remember a darling Chow cross. Chows are reported to be notorious for subtle body language. The only warning this girl gave before nipping was a flick of the ear. She was not a bad dog: she just was not giving the owners much to "read." The children were pushing her past her tolerance level and then the adults punished her harshly for "not giving warning." Do you want a breed or cross of one that is recognized for giving limited body language with a child? My feeling is no. This is why careful research and choice of the dog is vital.

Often herding dogs are not recommended for homes with children because it is feared the dogs will chase and nip at running kids. A properly raised herding breed living with children who learned how to behave with a dog, can make the difference between a dog learning to play safely with the little humans or deciding to round them up. I own Shelties (Shetland Sheepdogs, sometimes called Mini Collies), a breed often assumed as hyperactive and nippy with children. I have been around the breed all my life. Shelties from good sources and with dedicated owners can be superb companions for the children in the house. However, if you fail in your duties as a parent and dog owner, then your herding dog can become a nervous, hyper, nipping monster.

Many children beg for toy breeds or small dogs. However, many toy breeds can injure easily if a child should drop, fall or step on the dog. In addition, many children love to scoop up the dog like a toy. No matter how small, dogs are still dogs and not toys. A child swooping down and scooping the tiny pooch up can incite a bite. Eventually many dogs learn that becoming a tiny terror will get the kiddo to back down.

Giant breeds, though many can be very gentle, can easily topple a child. One swipe from a Mastiff's tail could send a toddler sprawling. A goofily bounding Great Dane pup can injure a child. Many large dogs may not realize just how big they are. Again, a properly raised big dog in the proper home can be a superb companion for the children. I have also had large dogs with infants and toddlers. Though, if the parents are not doing their work, then the results can be devastating.

The activity levels of many terrier breeds may be more than a parent can handle when combined with an active child. An active toddler constantly in motion and refusing to nap may be a lot for a parent to handle. Combine that with a dog possibly needing hours of quality activity can try even a saint's patience.

Sometimes the best dog for a child is that canine of undeterminable parentage. A good rescue group that has screened a dog carefully with children of various ages as well as tested the dog's tolerance level can help match your family with a great cross.

When choosing a dog for your child, you need to look at the age of your child, the needs of the dog, carefully researched breed traits (do not go by media hype or what the guy at the local corner pet supply store or even pet shop states) and determine if you can give each what they need.

There is no perfect age dog for a child. Puppies and adolescent dogs need more maintenance than adult dogs. Many parents find themselves overwhelmed with both a puppy and a young child. Parents with older children may have more time for a pup or adolescent dog (as long as they are not running all over creation between work, school activities and extracurricular activities). Adult dogs can be great companions for homes with children. However, you must make sure you get a dog that has been well socialized and has been treated nicely by children. Many dog-related issues are not really the fault of the dog. Often, it is a case of the parent not adequately choosing, raising, training, socializing and maintaining both dog and child.

There is no perfect age child for a dog, either. Many rescues and breeders will not place a dog in a home with an infant or young child. The younger the child, the more care is needed and less time is devoted to the dog. Young children may behave in ways that can rapidly push the tolerance level of a dog. Good rescues and breeders are just trying to prevent tragedy. This is not to say that you cannot make it work. Older children may intentionally do things that teach the puppy or dog undesired behaviors are GOOD things. I have consulted many a "problem" dog whose behaviors stemmed directly back to how the older children in the family interacted with the dog. You need to look at not only the needs of the dog but the needs of your children based on age when determining if a dog is even a good idea at this stage in your life. Please remember, factor in school events, sports, play dates, etc, when considering a dog. The less overall time you have to devote solely to the dog and children, the greater the potential for problems.

One of the most disturbing calls I ever received was from a family with several older children (middle and high school) and two in early elementary school. Mom and Dad both worked outside of the house. The children and dog were home alone for several hours every afternoon. The older children were teaching the dog to play dangerous games: games that included grabbing clothes, biting legs, dragging smaller children by their arms, jumping and knocking down the smallest. By the time I was called, the elementary school administrator had called in child protective services. The parents were spoken to prior to CPS being called, but the parents chose to ignore the situation. The youngest children were going to school with nasty bites and scratches. Child services gave the ultimatum of fix the situation or lose the children. Mom and Dad knew what the older children were doing but were not in a position to monitor their actions. Dad seemed to not think there was anything wrong with some "horseplay" between the older children and the dog. He felt the dog would stop biting when he got older. The dog's "training" from the children was biting is good! To add insult, the dog was an American Pit Bull Terrier. So we add a dog of a breed with a bad rap to a family with irresponsible parents and out of control teens who think biting is funny, two young children who are regularly injured and throw in a school administrator looking out for the safety of the children... Anyone should be able to see how this will turn out. Sadly, the father refused to work with the situation because he honestly thought the dog would grow out of the behaviors. Dogs do not spontaneously grow out of things without human intervention.

*****

Another family with a similar situation as above had a Beagle. Mom was a stay-at-home mom, but always on the go. She had a toddler at home and two older boys. Between various activities, sports, PTA, volunteering during the day, shopping, etc, her puppy got less quality time than many successful dog-owning people who worked full time. It was no wonder the puppy was developing significant issues. To complicate matters, the older boys encouraged the puppy to go after the toddler. Every time the pup started to play rough, the boys laughed, played back roughly. They encouraged clothes pulling, finger pulling, attacking feet, etc. All these human behaviors taught the pup that biting was good. It was a neat game according to one son: until the tot got a nasty play bite to his calf. Of course Mom blamed the pup. No matter how much I worked with the boys, mother and the pup, as soon as I left, Mom failed in her duties. The situation worsened, blood was drawn regularly and the pup relished in the game. Sadly, I later learned the family had given up a previous dog due to biting. Mom's excuse was "Well boys will be boys and what can I do?" Obviously her answer was to dump one dog and get another and not address the root of the biting: the children.

*****

Allyson had serious emotional issues and phobias. Her stress levels were extremely high and eventually her mother began homeschooling combined with a lot of psychological intervention. Allyson was open about her condition and was trying so hard. It is difficult enough being a teenage girl, add in emotional disorders, and it is even more complicated. Mom began watching how Allyson gravitated towards animals. Eventually, she and her husband decided to add a dog. They chose the breed and breeder with extreme care. They got a carefully chosen Golden Retriever. Allyson took to training like a duck to water. The dog flourished. Allyson began leaving the home, her stress levels lessened and she made friends. Allyson loved going to classes and began expanding her horizons. By now she is college age and I hope the basis Allyson received through dedicated parents and a well-chosen canine companion will see the young woman far.

The right dog for the right home with children can be a wonderful experience! However, adding a dog to a home with a child in residence, where a child will be added or even visit regularly requires careful consideration.

WHAT IS THE BEST DOG FOR A HOME WITH OTHER PETS?

Similarly, to a home with children, there is no perfect type of dog for a home with other pets. You need to evaluate your current pets. Consider temperaments, behaviors and acceptance of animals on and off their territory before bringing home a dog. Then you have to choose the best match of a dog for your environment. Along with this, you still have to look at other issues raised: time commitment, can you afford to add a dog, etc.

Caged pets may be easier to manage in some respects when adding a dog. It is easier to keep them separate from your new dog when you are not able to supervise. However, you still need to be diligent. Even when in a cage, a small pet may be injured or even killed if a dog tries to get in the cage. Baby gates and closed doors when you are not able to teach the dog desired behaviors is a must.

You must consider the background of the breed you are considering as well as the background of the individual dog. Breeds with a strong hunting drive, especially ones bred to hunt vermin, may not be the best choice if you have ferrets or house rabbits, for example. Not to say that dogs with a hunting backgrounds cannot live harmoniously in a home with small pets, but you need to remember the background of the dogs. The dogs and small animals must never be alone without proper and careful adult supervision. Careful integration and constant observation will be vital. Even with non-hunting breeds, the small animals in my house are in rooms that are gated off when no human is in the room.

I remember pet sitting for a Cairn Terrier. She was not raised as a terrier; instead she was being raised as a lap dog. I do not even think she had ever chased a squirrel. For the first few nights, she ignored my rabbits. Then her instincts kicked into gear and she began digging at the cages, barking at the rabbits and needed to be taught not to charge the cages. Even with that, it was a tense few more days. On the other hand, I grew up with a Scottie who was devoted to our guinea pigs, but all other rodents were fair game. My current dogs pretty much ignore our caged pets, even when the pets are out. However, they are always supervised carefully!

What if you have other pets such as cats and dogs or livestock that are not always separated by a cage? Again, be careful with your choice of new companion. For example, it is often said you cannot own a Greyhound or other sight hound if you have cats. This is false. A woman I knew recently adopted a rescue Greyhound who is doing superbly with her older cats. Work with good breeders or rescues and look for people who are socializing their animals to as many other animals as possible. Remember, no one can state if a particular dog is good with something if the dog has never been exposed to it: especially when dealing with an adult dog.

Do not risk a purchase or adoption if the dog has no known or a questionable history with other animals. It is not fair for you, your current pets or the dog. Scour the free pet lists and just see how many state "Got the dog from a friend, dog will not stop tormenting my cat/ferret/rabbit and the dog has to go (or the other pet has to go)." Being bounced from home to home is stressing on a dog. Stress can bring about undesired behaviors. Puppies may be easier to work with if they have not been exposed to say cats than an adult dog. If you start with a puppy and work for a happy integration from day one, you stand a better chance. It is possible to integrate an adult dog into a home with a cat. It is easier to do if the cat and dog have had prior good experiences with the other species in the past.

IS MY CURRENT PET READY FOR A NEW PUPPY OR DOG?

I have consulted with various owners who brought in new dogs when the current dog (or cat) had shown significant signs of aggressions and fears before the new dog was acquired. In one case, the new dog was eventually killed when the owner failed to follow my advice which was to immediately contact a behaviorist I recommended in her region (she contacted me from hours away). The owner took the cheap way out and followed bad advice acquired through the internet. Her new dog paid with his life. When the signs are there, do not ignore them.

Julia and Jake were a young, active couple. Jake was in federal law enforcement. They had an ancient and honorable dog of mixed heritage, possibly pit and Labrador. Abby was tolerant of dogs but liked her personal space. Julia and Jake had to place a puppy several years earlier because the old girl just would not accept him. From what I gathered, the other puppy was allowed to drive the old girl insane. Jake wanted to enter a canine division at work. Instead of waiting for the Abby to leave this plane (which was not much longer in the grand scheme of our lives with dogs) before the husband applied for a different position at work; the husband applied and rushed in a big, goony, adolescent, extremely active, working dog who was still in training. Abby was overwhelmed and miserable. She was beginning to attack the new dog every time he pounced on her. These attacks would affect the new dog's ability to work. After a solid evaluation and observations, I felt with a combination of work and management with both dogs, the situation could work. Abby was showing interest in the other dog but did not like it when he pounced. When the new dog was not harassing her, she relaxed and went about her own business. Abby began to accept him but the situation would need dedication and work. The question became would the owners do the work and while doing the work, how much of the new dog's working ability would be affected? This was a very unique situation.

Dogs may not show their adult temperament until two to three years of age when they are fully mature. The assumption that by a year old a dog is grown up is erroneous. At a year of age, the dog is an adolescent. Keep this in mind when looking at add a new dog.

Sofia was part of a litter surrendered to a local rescue. The situation was known to the rescue group. The mother was aggressive. Since the puppies looked and acted differently than the dam, they were placed for adoption. Sofia was in a very knowledgeable environment with experienced owners. A second dog was added while Sofia was a young adolescent. However, as Sofia matured, her inherited temperament began to show. Sofia went from a happy pup and adolescent going to dog parks, long walks, travelling and loving her younger canine companion to aggressively attacking him and other dogs. After extensive work with me and a request for a second opinion from a behaviorist to make sure I was not missing something, the couple contacted the rescue. Then we learned the sad fact that every puppy from that litter was either returned or euthanized for severe aggression before the age of two. The rescue staff blamed every home for failing the puppies. Now, given the fact that mom was dangerous and every puppy regardless of the environment developed aggressions as they neared full maturity, it is more likely that the puppies inherited the issues. The person I requested a second opinion from agreed with me about my diagnosis and what I had done. She recommended euthanizing. Behaviors are part heredity and part what is done with it. This is why people who seek breeders are told observe dogs related to the one being considered.

Sofia was not an isolated case. Another puppy I worked with was a happy guy as a baby but came from a mother who had severe fears. Dogs related to her were the same. Big red flags the buyer did not heed at the breeder: multiple related dogs with behavioral problems. The owner did work to try and overcome his background, but this boy inherited a predisposition for this behavior. I remember talking to a Fila Brasileiro breeder who was getting periodic calls from new puppy buyers from all over the US (she was involved with a national club) and the owners were upset that the puppies were too friendly. She could not get the owners to realize that it could take up to three years for the dogs to mature into what the breed description stated the breed should be AND the owners had to work hard to cultivate it into something manageable or else they would end up in over their heads.

There is a genetic component to temperament and training may not always overcome it. I cannot ask a Labrador Retriever to behave like a Caucasian Mountain Dog just like I cannot expect a Basset Hound to be a Border Collie.

When we ignore the hereditary component, we do dogs a disservice. Even within a breed or type of designer crossbred, you can have variations in inherited traits. There are no guarantees: you can only hope that the person placing the dogs is doing all he can to help ensure solid temperament within the breed standard. The better the parents are; the increased likelihood of that being passed on. With rescues, the background may be unknown. With pet stores, it is unknown. With breeders, you should have the chance to meet the dam. This will be discussed more later.

If your current pets are not suited for adding a dog, do not risk disaster. If you know an issue exists, why potentially make things worse? If in doubt, call in a trainer to perform some evaluations. However, if all is fine and you feel another dog can integrate into your home, you must now carefully choose the best match for your situation.

WHAT AGE DOG SHOULD I ADD?

Now that you have decided to add another dog to your home, what is the best age? It may be easier to introduce a puppy into a home with existing adult animals. Adult dogs may give puppies a bit more leeway with behaviors than they may adolescent or adult dogs. However, the antics of a young pup may be more than a senior pet can handle. It will be up to you to ensure that your puppy is properly introduced to the existing pet and given enough proper training and management so as not to become a nuisance. If you do not have the time to do this, reconsider adding another animal. Sometimes it may take weeks or longer to integrate a new puppy (or dog) into a home.

If you want to bring home an adult dog, ask the breeder or rescue if the dog has been around other dogs of various genders (both intact and altered), sizes and ages, what were the reactions and were any red flags observed. Ask if you can have your current dog meet the potential new dog on neutral territory, at the potential new dog's current home and then at your house. If your request is refused, do not consider the dog. There may be a behavioral reason that is being hidden. Ask a trainer or behavioral consultant to come along and observe the dogs together as there may be signals indicating issues that you and the foster care givers may not pick up. Adult dogs may have habits from the previous owner that will need working out. However, with an adult dog, there is no shock in regards to size, coat type, etc.

Look for a dog that will compliment but not be a challenge to current pets. Dogs that have not been good with cats or good with only specific cats should not come into a home with cats. It could be risky. If a dog has a history of chasing livestock, I would not advise this dog for a farm or life near farms, even if the dog would be confined. A dog that has shown aggression issues with other dogs may not integrate into a home with other dogs. If you have tiny dogs, should you consider bringing in a Great Dane? Even a misstep could seriously injure your

Toy Poodle. Many giant dogs live great with smaller dogs, but you need to choose carefully. Lastly, make sure your current pets (especially dogs) have a solid background with training, manners and socializing. Behaviors may regress with the addition of a new dog and you need to make sure your current dog is as prepared for the change as possible.

With puppies, serious breeders will not place before 8 weeks of age. There is a lot of growth and development between weaning and the first 12 weeks of age. Know local laws and avoid anyone placing puppies younger than (1) legal age and (2) eight weeks of age or so. Puppies placed too young will miss out on a lot of lessons that should help prepare the puppy for placement. Serious people will spend those weeks exposing the puppies to things and beginning to teach them how to be away from the dam and littermates. Some will even begin leash work, housetraining, crate training and basic manners. People who are placing puppies very young, even if they are orphaned, are not taking responsibility for placing the puppies with the best foundation possible.

TWO MAY NOT BE BETTER THAN ONE

Quite a few of my clients thought two puppies at once would be a good idea as the puppies could keep each other company when the owner was not around. Acquiring two puppies at the same time is a mistake for the average home. Two pups are more than double the work and expense. If you do not treat each puppy as an individual and give each pup ample time alone and socializing, the pups may bond closer to each other than to the humans. If the pups become security blankets for each other, being apart may become traumatizing. Also, they are developing at the same rate. They will hit milestones together and may scuff more than dogs with a bit of an age difference. It is a better idea to wait until one pup is older and has the training and socializing foundation you want, then add a second dog.

Jessica and her husband were very experienced, small dog owners. Jessica had retired and her husband was considering it in the near future. They knew how to prevent the issues many small dog owners create (often called "Small Dog Syndrome.") However, Jessica decided that this time, she would get two puppies. They had an older dog and wanted the pups to help ease the pain of the older girl's all too foreseeable passing (poor health) and to give the pups a playmate so the older dog would not be the focus of puppy antics. The puppies were not littermates but were purchased from a local designer dog breeder who always has puppies available. I was called in as soon as the pups came into the home. The pups were quite different in activity levels. Jessica, main caregiver, was overwhelmed because as one pup tired, the other turned to the senior dog for play.

Over the next few weeks, we changed how the pups were managed so each got time alone and time together. The pups were walked together and after the lower energy one was done, he went home for a nap and higher energy pup went for a longer walk. Then this pup took a nap and other pup was taken out. They were played with together and as one tired, this pup would take a nap and then individual play time was given. During these times, formal manners were taught as a team and individually. Over the next 18 months, I was randomly called in to tweak things as the puppies reached various developmental milestones. The husband would help out when he was home so the pups and the senior dog had all needs met.

Jessica and her husband said it was a lot of work. Once they got into a routine, the puppies learned the rules of the house and had bonded with the humans closer than to each other, things became much easier. However, never again would they take on two puppies at once with what they now knew!

CHAPTER FOUR

WHERE AND HOW SHOULD I CHOOSE MY DOG?

Once you have determined that you are ready for a dog and can make all the commitments a dog will need, your next big decision is the source of your dog. I only recommend two sources: a rescue or a serious breeder.

The discussion of rescue or breeder is very touchy. Some people feel anyone should be able to breed dogs regardless of the motives. Others want tight restrictions on breeding. Some scream rescue only while others will insist you use a breeder as a good breeder will do various testing and cautious breeding. **The choice is yours.** Let us take a look at various sources people choose for dogs.

RESCUES

There are different kinds of rescues. For the purpose of this, I am going to break down rescues to two main areas: Kennels (public or private shelters) and Foster Homes (using foster homes with no kennel facility), some rescues may use a combination of kennels and foster homes. There are varying degrees within each when it comes to how and what dogs they place. When considering a rescue dog, research the pros and cons of each type of rescue. For example: In kennel situations, it may not be as easy for the staff to evaluate the dogs, if they do at all. There is only so much that can be done in a room with controlled situations. Say under controlled situations, the rescue feels a dog exhibits moderate animal aggression. How will the dog behave in the "real world?" The dog could escalate to severe animal aggression in a situation where the owner cannot control how an approaching dog is managed. People fostering dogs have the dogs in a real world environment, therefore, should be able to identify and work with issues before placing a dog. Alternatively, at a fostering home, the dog may be comfortable and not show undesired behaviors. Dogs behave differently in their comfort zones than when in stress zones. Not all foster families will properly work through behavioral issues. How the foster family works with the dog will affect future behavior. It is possible the foster family has done things that give the appearance of improvement behaviorally. However, in reality, the foster family was working the dog in a way that increased anxiety and the behaviors will return with a sudden explosion after adopting such as punishing stress-related behaviors such as fears, aggressions, lunging, barking, etc. Now let us look a little closer at rescues.

KENNEL TYPE shelters vary from outstanding to minimal care warehouses. Kennel type rescues may be public or private. Some are able to give dogs every chance before considering euthanasia while others cannot afford that luxury. Some will not euthanize, but may be very specific about what dogs they accept or turn away. Some may even turn away adoptable dogs so they can take on only hard cases for which adoption may not be viable/safe option. It is possible to find a wonderful dog at a kennel type shelter if you use common sense. Some of the best dogs I have ever worked with came from kennel type shelters: both public and private.

A public shelter often takes in every dog. Sometimes, owner-surrender dogs go on the adoption floor based solely on what the surrendering party claims. Sadly, it is not uncommon for surrendering owners to downplay or lie about behavioral issues because they want to give their dog every chance at a home. This is understandable, though it means there is a chance a significant concern could be passed on to an unsuspecting person. Not all dogs given up have behavioral issues. Many are from owners who got a dog on impulse and cannot keep the poor thing. Others are from owners who had a baby and decided child and dog were too much work. Some owners have had major life changes and the dog is now neglected so the owner chooses to try and give the dog a chance at a better life. I ran into a woman who wanted to give up her dog because he was shy and she was renovating her townhouse. Having a dog while dealing with home renovations was more than the owner wanted to handle. The dog was actually quite sweet. Some give up puppies because they are too much work. Others give up dogs because they get too big or too hairy or bark or did not housetrain in seven days like that book promised and even because the dog no longer matches the new décor.

While in a kennel, not all dogs will exhibit the behaviors for which they were surrendered. It is not the shelter staff's fault if an owner lies on the forms and the dog does not exhibit the concerning behaviors. Things such as housetraining and chewing may not be readily discernable in a cage. Even some aggressions may not manifest in a shelter. This should not stop you from considering a public shelter. Instead, do not rely solely on the reason for surrender when choosing a dog. Gather as much information as you can about the dog before you say "yes." You could save a wonderful life and adopt a great dog!

Before I continue, I have to say: please, do not refuse to go to a shelter because the staff may have to euthanize animals. Shelters do not do this because they are heartless. Pets in shelters are a sad reality of irresponsible owners. What happens to the dogs a "no-kill" rescue turns away due to lack of space or because the dogs are too big, too old or even the wrong type? Some of them end up being abandoned, even on the shelter property. This happened several times during the years I worked at a "no-kill" shelter when we refused to take dogs when the shelter was at capacity or because the intake coordinator felt the dog was not a good candidate for fast adoption. Some of the dogs raced into the fields behind the shelter. Another died on the busy street in front of the shelter (he died in my arms after being hit by a car). The luckier ones went to the "kill shelter" up the street where, if not placed, at least they had a humane euthanasia. However, it is also your responsibility not to jump at a dog because you know he faces euthanasia. I know it hurts, and I have been there myself. You need to make the best choice in all fairness to your family and the dog.

Many of the worst matches I have worked with came from people who felt bad because a dog was nearing his end at a shelter but chose to ignore significant signs the match would not work. There may be a reason the dog has not been placed. Possibly the dog was surrendered with a behavior that most adopters are not able to safely manage let alone successfully work through. It is possible the dog has been at the shelter so long he has developed undesired issues that turn away many adopters. Long term kenneling at a shelter is psychologically stressing. It is possible the dog can be brought around with a little work. It is also possible that so much damage has been done prior to surrender and at the shelter that the dog is too far gone for the average home to safely handle. Some shelters would rather euthanize a dog that has no hopes of placement so they can help other dogs. If the unadoptable dog is kept, they may have to turn away dozens of dogs if not more during the life of the unadoptable dog. Alternatively, someone may place the unadoptable dog and the result could be tragic. Let us look a bit closer at the dogs.

Is that dog appearing quiet in his run really calm and sedate? It is possible that the dog is so terrified he is frozen with fear. That dog barking maniacally at the gate may not be aggressive. He may be frustrated or overly excited. Runs can be a difficult place in which to see the best, or worst, in a dog. When you see a dog you are interested in, ask if a staff member can take the dog out of the run and to an area away from the other dogs. See how the dog reacts. Look for body language cues that could indicate what may be going on: is the tail set high and stiff or is it tucked way under the bottom or is it wagging happily? Are the dog's ears pinned back tight against the head, pitched way forward or held in a relaxed manner? It the dog on his toes, hackles raised or is he lip licking and avoiding gazes? Does he appear hyper-vigilant, terrified or relaxed? Is his whole body tense or is he easy going? There are many subtle cues to look at. If you are in doubt of your abilities to read a dog, ask a local trainer to come with you. You may have to pay a fee for the trainer's time, but it may be the difference between a life of fun or one of stress. Bear in mind, this is still no 100% guarantee of a great dog choice, but it is important to read that dog the best you can.

There is a liability issue with knowingly placing dogs with dangerous behaviors. Anyone working with dogs must realize this. Some shelters have staff and volunteers who are very cautious about this while others do not. If owners were more responsible and did their jobs, fewer dogs would end up unwanted. Some rescues will not euthanize a dog at all, regardless of the reason for surrender and what they witness. This has lead to a more than a few truly dangerous dogs being placed. Shelters are put in a bad situation when it comes to what they take in, should they euthanize and what is a good candidate for adoption. Not all shelter staff will use common sense. Just because we want every unwanted dog to have a home, there may not be a home suited for every dog. Alternatively, do not pass up a dog due only to age. Some of the best matches I have worked with were senior dogs given a second chance.

Once you have found a dog you are interested in, ask to review all forms pertaining to the dog, including any evaluations. How do the evaluations compare with the surrender information and what the adoption counselor says? As a potential adopter, remember behavioral evaluations only look at the behavior at that given time on that given day. I have evaluated dogs whose owners claimed significant behavioral issues and I was unable to get the behaviors to reproduce. It happens. Has the shelter done more than one evaluation and how do the results compare? Formal evaluations are often done in more controlled environments than an owner will face "real world." If a dog is giving concerning behaviors in a controlled evaluation, there is a chance the behaviors will be worse when faced with a similar situation in an uncontrolled environment.

What the dog has been exposed to prior to the evaluation could skew the readings. Was an "Assess-a-Hand" (fake hand on a stick) used? A dog who has been hit with a stick in the past may not evaluate well when he sees that stick with a funny smelling, fake hand coming at him. A doll will not elicit the same response from a dog as a real child. Evaluations are designed to mimic what a dog may experience but are not 100% accurate for many reasons.

Some evaluators are overly aggressive, pushing a dog to the breaking point. I have seen videos of dogs inhumanely poked and prodded with an Assess-a-Hand for many minutes before reacting with a quick growl, a snap and then walking away, and the evaluator failed the dogs. Dogs may have gender-specific aggressions or fears. How does the dog respond to both genders? Some evaluators forget breed traits with evaluations. A Golden Retriever will not evaluate the same as a Shetland Sheepdog which will not evaluate the same as a Jack Russell Terrier which will not evaluate the same as a Chow Chow. Overall evaluations are only as good as the person doing the evaluating. I am not saying you should discount an evaluation. The evaluation can provide decent information when combined with information given at time of surrender. If the dog was a stray or a confiscation, evaluations and observation are the only references you have.

If the rescue refuses for any reason to allow you to see the documents, do not adopt the dog. If you are told there is personal information on some forms so you cannot see them, ask the staff to cover the personal info and make a copy. Again, you deserve to see the forms. If you are stonewalled, ask to speak to a supervisor and explain why you will not be adopting a dog from them. There is a chance the adoption counselor is not following protocol in order to get a dog moved. There is a chance you may get protocols changed. In the end, not being able to review forms prior to adopting is denying you vital information so you can make the most educated decision possible.

Do not forget to ask about medical issues. As with behavioral issues, shelter staff may be at the mercy of what the surrendering owner says. Some groups may have dogs fully vetted and try to check for underlying conditions. Others do not have the budget. Do not blame the staff if something was left off by the surrendering owner. Not all medical issues will be readily apparent. It is possible for a dog with a medical condition to be adopted and the shelter unaware. If the staff is aware of an issue, ask for information on it. Many conditions are treatable or manageable. Ask if the dog was spayed (it is easy to tell if a male has been neutered). Again, shelters may have to go by what the surrendering owner claims. If there is a veterinarian listed on surrender forms, ask if the shelter can call to verify surgery. If not and you choose to adopt the dog, ask your vet to help you determine if she was spayed or not. There have been cases of pregnant dogs being surrendered with the staff told the dog was spayed. I have had more than one call from people who adopted dogs and a couple weeks later: PUPPIES!

After you adopt the dog, no matter what you are told, have the dog examined by your own veterinarian as soon as possible after adoption and enroll in a good training program. After making the most educated decision possible regarding your new dog, a good veterinarian and good trainer will be your best allies.

Please, do not let what you have read deter you from looking at a shelter. Just go in with your eyes open and your homework done. Not all Shelters are equal. Adopting a dog is a serious undertaking and you need all the information possible so you can make an education decision. You could end up finding the dog of your dreams in that scruffy little thing. Many of my clients have!

Mickey was from a local shelter. Her adopters had researched dog body language, talked to people about what to look for and checked out each dog they were interested in very carefully. She was shy in her cage, but once out of the shelter and walking on the lawns, she was a completely different animal. Mickey was a fun little dog with a love of learning.

*****

Lola was adopted from the same shelter as Mickey. Her surrendering owner claimed on the documents that she was sweet, loved children, adored everyone, however due to human illness, keeping Lola was not an option. Lola's adopters were experienced dog owners. Within a day after adopting, Lola was snarling at the children, lunging at people and behaving in a very disturbing manner not witnessed at the shelter. Her adopters got a full vet check and a referral to me. As I took a history, I learned the new owners had only gone by what the surrender forms indicated and never took Lola from her cage. Lola was quiet in the cage but did not respond to people. After extensive work, veterinary workups and continuous worsening of the issues, it was determined that there was something pretty significant going on with Lola and she was euthanized.

Again, do not let this deter you from adopting from a shelter. Instead, use this as a reason to do your homework and carefully check out each dog the best you can.

Now we will move on to rescue groups that use foster homes.

FOSTER HOME RESCUES attracted many of my clients. They decided to go with rescues that used exclusively foster homes assuming the dogs would get some form of training, socializing and good evaluations before adoption. Many rescues do a good job of all these things, but some do far more harm than good.

I was at an adoption fair observing a rescue team with whom I was very familiar. The director frequently called me or referred adopters to me regarding behavioral issues with foster and newly adopted dogs, especially crate issues. I was curious so I started observing their adoption fairs. I watched several volunteers try to quiet dogs that were expressing stress (barking, whining) by spraying them in the face with water. Allegedly they had been instructed to do this because it would work! Yes, the dogs stopped barking, but started up again in a few minutes. The water spray increased the stress levels of the dogs. The helpers at the fair escalated to yelling at the dogs and even banging the crate tops. The crates were becoming places of behavioral torture. I witnessed this on various occasions. It is stressing enough for a dog to be at an adoption fair without the volunteers making it worse. Many dogs stopped the behaviors so the director assumed the harsh training worked. However, it worked for the wrong reasons. The dogs were suppressing body language but still in high-stress mode. Nothing was done to help the dog associate adoption fairs with good things. The dogs were never given a chance to develop good crating manners and learn to feel a crate was safe. How would the dogs behave the next adoption fair? What undesired behaviors and fears were being passed on to unsuspecting adopters? Many of these dogs developed serious crate aggressions in their new homes. The dogs learned not to show these behaviors while in foster and at fairs in order to avoid punishment; however, once adopted, the behaviors exploded.

As with working with a kennel style rescue, you need to observe the dog's body language as well as how the fostering family interacts with the dog. Look and listen for red flags. For example, the dog is supposedly great with children, but the foster home has no children. You notice the dog backing away, tail tucked, whites of eyes showing, and ears pinned, from your well-behaved child. The foster home tells you the dog is just shy. Should you adopt the dog? I would not. Do you have cats? Has the dog ever been exposed to cats and what was the reaction? If the foster home does not have a cat, ask if there is a way you can see the dog with a cat. Ask the fosterer to take the dog for a walk with you. How does the dog behave and what excuses does the fostering family make? Ask what work has been or is being done with the dog. Ask it to be demonstrated and how do you feel? Is the dog showing stress at other dogs or pedestrians (barking and lunging) being punished for it or is the fosterer redirecting the dog and trying to teach the dog to relax? Does the fostering family state the dog needs a prong collar or head halter in order to be walked? You will learn a lot through observation. A dog that is punished to "get him through stress" is a dog developing worse issues.

Ask about medical issues. If the dog has been seen by a vet, ask if you can contact the vet for more information. You need to know if what the foster giver is doing is in agreement with the vet. If the dog has not been seen, ask why.

As with a kennel style rescue, ask to see ALL the paperwork and evaluations on the dog. Do not accept "Oh the director keeps all those and you will get them later after you adopt." You deserve to see the papers before making your choice. Ask to keep a copy of your adoption interview form. If it is done online, print a copy for yourself before hitting the send button. Compare what you said with what the dog's file says. You state clearly you have other pets or are considering starting a family and may discover the person handling the adoption tries to hand you a dog that has not been exposed to other animals, children or not good with either. Why is the person trying to adopt this dog to you? Rescues that are not trying to make the best matches are rescues to avoid. On the other hand, some rescues do an outstanding job of bringing in and rehabilitating dogs.

Dusty was from a good owner but the human's life had changed and the owner had to move back with family. The extended family was turning Dusty into a behavioral wreck. I did the initial intake evaluation and found a dog that enjoyed being handled, had a lot of tolerance, but if not out of that situation soon, he would worsen. A regularly visiting special needs child was allowed to hit him when the owner was not present. The extended family felt Dusty should tolerate a big child smacking him. Dusty's owner was trying to find a new home and new work, but had no idea how long it would take. She felt Dusty needed a better chance at the life she tried to provide. I outlined a plan of rehabilitation with the foster care giver and I handled the passing on of Dusty to her. Dusty came around and was a new dog last I heard.

As with shelters, do not let this deter you from considering adopting from a rescue that uses foster homes. Do your homework and go in as educated as possible while you make your choice. You may adopt a superb dog that will bring you years of enjoyment.

IS THIS REALLY A RESCUE? Another issue I must raise, as this seems to be becoming a bit more common, is that the rescue is not truly a rescue. Instead, they are doing only "courtesy listings" for owners who have dogs they must re-home. There are no foster homes, no evaluations, nothing by the "rescue." Ironically, some of these "rescues" will do a home check and ask for an adoption form to be filled out and some may even take a fee. Talk to the rescue coordinator and ask why there are so many "courtesy listings" for private owners. Ask if anyone from the club or group visits the dogs for evaluations. If not, this is a red flag. The adopter is at the mercy of the honesty of the current owner. Sadly, remember, the owner wants to get rid of the dog and this may lead to misrepresentations of said animal. Do you think the owner will honestly tell you if the dog is a risk?

One of my most memorable clients was from a "courtesy listing" rescue. The rescue was part of a regional breed club. Adopters are put through a home check and fill out an adoption form. However, there is no provision for a dog to be returned to the rescue as there is no true rescue. The "foster homes" are the surrendering homes and the dogs, at least at the time of writing, are not evaluated at all.

The adopter was never told this was how the club ran the rescue. This bit of vital information was placed well after the available dogs list, adoption application and adoption costs, where the average viewer would no look. The adopter was never told the rescue was not really a rescue when the club representatives performed a home check. During my initial evaluation of the issues, a few things the owner stated made no sense; I decided to check the club's website. This dog may never rehabilitate. The owner is highly dedicated and knowledgeable in the breed and is realistic. She contacted the former owner and learned that the poor boy was beaten and not fed as punishments. Last session we had, she was fighting to get the club to be more forthcoming with their information and have the dogs evaluated. Had this dog gone into a different home, things could have been far worse. The rescue was absolved of everything because of the fine print, hidden way at the bottom. In retrospect, the adopter thinks the dog was terrified to show anything in the home when she went to meet him. He just hung there, quietly. Had the dog gone to a foster home, the behaviors would have come out. The dog exhibited the behaviors from the moment he entered the adopting home.

Next, is the rescue truly a non-profit rescue? There are people claiming to be rescues that are actually using this guise as a way to sell animals and support themselves. The animals receive minimal care with the majority of the money used to line the pockets of the "rescuer." Look for red flags and ask questions. Does the person have many animals and not one assisting foster home? If so, ask why. Does what is indicated on the website appear to be real when you enter the home? Does the rescue take in animals from the local pound? If so, call the pound and see if they are one of the approved rescues they contact. Some public facilities have rescue groups to whom they may or may not release animals. Are the people bringing in dogs from different rural shelters all over and refusing to take in local dogs? Look to see if the rescue has any tax-exempt status. There are various forms of this with one of the more common being the 501(c) 3. Listen for key words such as "We are working on it." This may be true or they may not be. If you do not see anything on a website or in writing on an adoption contract, ask if the answer is "Yes," then get the tax-exempt number. If the rescue is new, it can take time to obtain non-profit status. Ask if paperwork has been filed. If the rescue is smart, they will have copies of what was filed with the IRS and when. If the person is running a non-profit without the proper documentation, this can come back to bite you and them in the tail. The person may also be gathering animals from free lists or even adopting them cheaply from pounds and later reselling. If in doubt, there are many other rescues from which you can choose.

NO ONE WANTS POOR MOLLY! A concern with all rescues, kennel or foster type, are the "guilt trip" placements. These ones really worry me. "Molly has been here for so long and no one wants her." Why does no one want Molly? There may be a legitimate reason such as Molly has more issues than the average home should sanely be expected to handle. It is your duty to ask or try to determine why the dog has been there for so long. Think hard, is this something with which you can sanely live and work through. Talk to trainers regarding the behaviors. Ask if the rescue will allow you to have a trainer look at the dog if you are very serious about the placement.

Sometimes, a dog being in a rescue for a long time is a case of the dog being a healthy, well-behaved senior and people do not want to deal with the inevitable within the next few years. Senior dogs have a lot to offer! Maybe the dog has a treatable medical issue or needs daily medication but since many want perfect animals, the dog is overlooked. Not all adopters are willing to pay for treatment, even if the cost is low. If this is something you feel comfortable managing and affording while the dog is a good candidate otherwise, maybe this is the dog for you.

Sometimes, the rescue has a dog that should not be placed. Some dogs are just too dangerous to sanely and safely adopt out. Some rescues assume every dog must find a home and ignore safety. Sadly, this leads to some bad situations.

Along with guilt trip placements are the downplaying of your concerns. Does the rescue appear to do this? Are you told just go buy "X" training device (often a head halter or even electric shock or prong collar) and the dog will be fine? Why can the dog not be managed without a device that helps prevent certain behaviors and may worsen others? If you see the potential for severe issues based on documentation with observation and the rescue does not seen to have the same concerns, why? I have observed rescue groups tell a potential owner that the dog was just a little stressed when the dog's body language was screaming something much different. This was not a little stress. This was a dog in a total panic. If your concerns are not taken seriously or you do not feel they are should you go through with the adoption?

Rocky's surrendering owner was quite honest when filling out his paperwork. Rocky had a three-year, documented history of significant aggressions including dog attacks and bites to people. Rocky had been worked with by at least one other trainer before surrender. His owners were military and had three dogs. Sadly, this move they were told they could only take two dogs. Therefore, they decided to give up the dog that was the most risk.

The rescue organization (private shelter) had Rocky evaluated twice in controlled situations and determined he showed moderate to serious dog aggression issues. In a real-life situation where the owner has no control of a situation, the reactions could become serious to extreme. Rocky was also showing willingness to redirect aggressions towards humans during the evaluations. The adoption counselors downplayed the red flags, placed Rocky in the exact type of home the evaluators recommended against and then told the adopters that a little training would do the trick. When I read the evaluation reports, I knew this was far from true. The impression I got from the evaluations was Rocky should have been euthanized but the shelter was no kill. To add to all this, Rocky was showing serious problems in the new home and the owners were physically unable to control him on walks, in a dog-dense region. Within weeks, Rocky was a severe danger to his community. It was not a case of if he bit but when and how severe the mauling would be. Rocky was one of a scant few dogs I recommended the owners consider euthanizing. He never should have been placed. I consulted with other dog professionals regarding his case and the owners later divulged they had contacted other trainers. Not one would take Rocky on because he was so dangerous. Rocky was a "guilt" adoption. He had been at the shelter for months and "No one wants him but he deserves a home," was the line given. The adopters never saw the documents about Rocky until after adoption.

Regardless of the kind of rescue you decide to work with, it is your duty to remember the following:

- ➤ It is your job to research what the best canine match would be for you. Do not go by what you see in the media or what an adoption counselor states. Talk to trainers, check out breed specific rescues and breed club websites, get your hands on books, etc. Knowing what the breed or breeds in the cross were developed for will help you decide what type of dog you should consider.
- ➤ Check out the rescue. Visit and talk to people before you are ready to fill out the paperwork. What is your first impression of the people you may be working with?
- ➤ Learn basic dog body language. Talk to trainers and ask for some red flags to consider. Turid Rugaas, Dr Ian Dunbar, Dr Karen Overall, Temple Grandin and Jean Donaldson all have excellent pieces you can find online regarding dog body language, as well as books and videos.
- ➤ If needed, consider asking a trainer to come help look at dogs with you and give you some tips on body language. A good trainer should not choose the dog for you but should help teach you what to look for. A great trainer will understand body language also how our body language affects what the dog does.
- ➤ Ask to see all paperwork for the dog prior to adoption. Check out the surrender form, any evaluations, medical concerns, etc. Do not blindly go by what you are told by the person handling the adoption.

- Do not let the rescue staff bully or guilt trip you into an adoption. For example, if you are told there is a wait list for the dog but you can take him now if you would like, ask to see the list to prove it. If there is a list of people interested, why is the list not being gone through in order of approved application now that the dog is cleared for adoption? Public shelters often do not hold dogs and adoption is on a first come, first adopt basis. Others may be trying to get the dog out and giving you a line.
- Make sure the rescue is truly a rescue and not someone gathering animals for resale under the guise of adoption, someone placing animals he bred using the word adoption to give the impression of a rescued litter or a courtesy listing service using the guise of rescue.

One word about adoption fairs: they are very stressing for dogs and it is tough for a rescue to evaluate adoptive homes in such an environment. Fairs are an excellent way to get visibility for their animals, but you should have the ability to see the dog you are interested in adopting in a more neutral area. A rescue should not let you take the dog home that day. They should insist on taking an application, putting you in line and contacting you to set up a more formal interview and evaluation of you and the dog for suitability.

When working with any rescue, be patient. Educate yourself well and be willing to keep checking for the best match for you. Since many rely on volunteers, if your first attempts at contact are not responded to, try again in a few days. Be patient. If you are considering adopting from a public or private kennel type shelter in which you should head down, check what they have available and do this weekly.

I have adopted many wonderful pets through both public shelters, private shelters and other rescues. I also adopted my hardest to manage dog through a private rescue (why he was in rescue to begin with). Rescue is rewarding and I know I am saving two lives: the pet I take in and the unwanted one who can now fill the open slot. It is also possible to find a wonderful competition dog. Both the American and United Kennel Clubs have provisions for crossbred dogs to compete in certain sports.

Just because an animal is in rescue does not mean there is a serious issue with the dog. Sometimes the behaviors are things that can be worked through. Some dogs are given up simply because the owners got bored, lacked time, new landlord, move, new child, new pet, new spouse or the dog simply got too old.

Finding a rescue is as easy as an internet search. PetFinder.com is a super resource listing thousands of rescues. Note, PetFinder.com does not clear or screen any of the rescues listed. Some are not even legitimate rescue groups. Sadly, I have had many clients end up getting dogs through people who were collecting them off free lists and posting them with a PetFinder.com page that made them appear to be legitimate rescue groups. Check out the rescues carefully.

You can also do an internet search for purebred rescues and dog clubs if this is the route you wish to take. Quite a few purebred dog clubs also support and have rescue information available to the public. Many rescues network so if there is no resource listed locally, contact the closest ones and ask for assistance. Some rescues advertise adoption events in local newspapers. You can also ask veterinarians, trainers and dog groomers or visit local dog shows for information on finding what you want in rescue.

BREEDERS

Technically anyone breeding dogs for whatever purpose can be called a breeder. Some breed for the betterment of a breed by health testing all dogs they are breeding and competing to prove the dogs are good breed representatives. They choose potential sires for litters carefully and have solid knowledge of bloodlines, genetics and health. They get out and prove the dogs have form and function by competing in various events or placing in homes that compete. They breed to a breed standard and know it inside and out. Never will a puppy be sold through a pet store or placed through a third party (broker). Good breeders will have a written contract outlining expectations of the owner. The contract should cover topics such as spaying or neutering, health guarantee (should clearly define what will be covered or not and be for the life of the dog) and what will happen if the owner cannot keep the dog. Good breeders have a lifetime investment in any animal produced by them. They want you to call if you have an issue or worry. Their reputation is at stake as well as the lives of the dogs they are placing.

Other breeders just breed dogs without taking serious steps in regards to health, proper temperament for the breed, etc. These breeders may say they are breeding for the love and betterment of a breed but are not doing so. A breeder cannot help better a breed if at least necessary health testing for the breed is not done. Some breed designer mutts. These are crossbred dogs given cutesy names and bred solely for making money. These breeders may tout erroneous information regarding hybrid vigor. Many health issues are common in many breeds that are very easy for a cross to inherit and/or pass genes into a new generation. Even if the produced puppies are not affected, they can be carriers of the undesired genes. These breeders may have a minimal contract with a short (a few days to even a couple years) guarantee, but for the most part: out of sight, out of mind once your check has cleared the bank. They have no true interest in whatever they are breeding, at least not like that of a dedicated breeder honestly trying to improve the quality of the breed.

Some breeders breed for retail sale. Since they wholesale animals to brokers and / or stores (and sometimes directly to the public) their incentive is to keep their overhead as low as possible, breed as many animals as possible and move the puppies as soon as possible. This means no showing or competing to prove the dogs fit the standard. There is no care to proper temperament of the dog bred and a pup's basis in temperament comes from the parents' genes. Limited health care above and beyond what is required by state law or to ship (and sometimes all the vaccines are given before the pup is even six weeks of age), and minimal physical care is given to the breeding dogs.

Only you can determine what the quality of breeder with whom you wish to work. Do you want to better the chances of a healthy dog or run the risk of a haphazardly bred animal?

How do you go about finding a breeder? One of the best ways is through dog clubs. You can find information about various dog clubs through the major registries, an online search and by visiting dog shows. Since serious breeders are working to better breeds and breed out health issues, they will often belong to clubs. A good club will have a code of ethics they expect all members to follow. This should outline things such as health tests, placing of animals, etc. Please note that registries are not clubs; individual breeders cannot be members of the American Kennel Club or the United Kennel Club. However, the registries have member clubs under their umbrellas and individuals are members of these clubs.

Not all registries are the same. Many have cropped up to give false credibility to less than ethical breeders who have lost privileges with more legitimate registries. Some less than ethical breeders can maintain the minimum standards required for registries and will do so. Registration is NOT a guarantee of health or quality. All registration means is the breeder has met the minimum requirements for the animal to be registered. Even with some registries trying to make it less desirable for lesser breeders to register dogs, many lesser breeders still decide to meet the requirements. It is up to the buyer to research and investigate the breeder.

Now to further complicate things, some breeds such as the Australian Shepherd and Border Collie have their own specific, legitimate, registries. However, there are also breed specific registries that were developed to give false credibility to designer mutts. How do you know if a registry is legitimate or not? Go by your instinct, look at registration requirements for dogs, events held, etc.

If you reside in the United States, you want to start your search with the American Kennel Club, United Kennel Club and Canadian Kennel Club. From there you can search for various member clubs within the registry. If you are outside the US, start a search with the national registry in your country.

In the United States, and in many other countries as well, beneath the umbrella of registries are national parent clubs for various breeds. For example, under the AKC, the parent club for the Shetland Sheepdog is the American Shetland Sheepdog Association. These national clubs can help you locate other local breed specific clubs in your region or help you find breeders closer to you.

Also under the registries are "multiple breed clubs." These clubs will have members who have dogs of various breeds as opposed to being dedicated to just one.

Breeders will network so if there is no club in your region, contact the closest one and see if they can assist. Many clubs have a formal breeder referral network.

Another way to find breeders is by visiting dog shows. Just remember that shows can be stressing for humans so do not expect to be able to sit and have long chats or handle dogs. Instead, buy a catalog that will list owners in the back. Ask people for cards so you can contact them later in the week. Be respectful of the intensity of dog shows for those competing.

Other sources for finding a breeder are trainers, veterinarians and word of mouth.

Once you have found a breeder, it is up to you to determine how ethical and serious the person is.

A few things to ask about are:

- What is the goal of the breeding program? Serious breeders will have a goal for their program that should include show and/or performance/working ability and health.
- What health issues are prevalent in the breed and for what have the sire and dam been tested? This will vary breed to breed so make sure you have this information before asking breeders about their particular dogs. Serious breeders will test for whatever is prevalent in the breed that can be tested for, epilepsy, for example, has **no** test or screening at this time.
- What titles have the parents and various relatives (on and off the pedigree) of the dogs won or are they being worked towards titles?
- Can you see the dam? If you cannot for any reason, be suspicious. This may be a broker or the dam may have temperament issues the seller does not want you to see. Many breeders seek outside stud dogs. If breeders only breed to their own studs or studs of a particular person only, be wary.
- What is the asking price of the puppies? Be cautious of anyone selling pups without pedigrees or registration for less than pups with these documents. Look price discrepancies between genders, if only some puppies are registered and of breeders asking far more or less than other breeders. Never hesitate to ask why.
- What contract do they offer? Better breeders will guarantee puppies for longer than just a few weeks as they know that many health issues such as epilepsy may not show up until the dog is a few years old. Short health guarantees, insisting on a specific veterinarian, insisting you breed or show the dog if you are looking for a pet, etc., are all red flags. A serious breeder will have a solid written contract clearly outlining the expectations of the owner.

- Will the breeder take the pup back at any point in time for any reason? Serious breeders will insist they are contacted if you can no longer keep your dog. They understand sometimes life throws us curves and they do not want dogs they were responsible for bringing into this world to end up in a rescue.
- What socializing and work has the breeder done before placing the puppies? It is amazing what young puppies can learn. Serious breeders will bring in visitors, expose puppies to different surfaces, sights, sounds and smells. Really serious breeders will begin leash work, crate training and getting puppies used to being separated for short time from their littermate and dam. Serious breeders know they set the foundation from which the owners build.

A few red flags:

- A breeder who is not competing with dogs, working with or producing dogs who are competing and who cannot show proof of titles awarded. However, this is not the only thing to look for, there are breeders breeding mainly for pets who do make sure they are performing extensive health testing and breeders who compete with their dogs but do no testing of breeding dogs.
- A breeder who insists all dogs are healthy and no testing is needed. However, with certain issues, if a parent is genetically clear, the offspring will be clear.
- A breeder who insists that working dogs do not need testing for things like hip dysplasia. Dogs may not show lameness with Hip Dysplasia.
- A breeder who always has puppies available or seems to be working with many breeds at once. However, some breeders who are also professional handlers may have various breeds on the premises that are clients' dogs.
- Breeders who say if they do not have what you want, they can acquire it (broker it) for you.
- Breeders who are creating designer dogs (crossbreds with a funky or cutesy name such as Shih-chons, Dalimers, Labradoodles or Puggles).
- Breeders who claim no one has better dogs.
- Breeders who sell young puppies as definite show/working quality.
- Breeders who will only show you one puppy in a litter and will not let you see the others.
- Breeders who will not allow you to see the parents (though not all breeders have the sire on premises, many will used outside dogs to help improve their lines) or other dogs they have.
- Breeders who only breed to their own dogs or only to dogs of close friends.

What health testing should you ask about? This will vary breed to breed. At minimum, a breeder should be checking hips and eyes (OFA and CERF). Then it is up to you to know the major issues in a breed, what has a genetic test and what just has a screening. For example, as of writing, there is no genetic test for hip dysplasia. However, there is a genetic test for von Willebrand's (a bleeding disorder) so if both parents are clear then the offspring will be clear. A breeder should be aware of the major health issues in the breed and you should not hesitate to "feel out" the knowledge of the breeder.

A dear friend of mine bought a lovely German Shepherd Dog puppy from a breeder. In hindsight, she never should have used the breeder: there were several red flags. Not long after purchase, the pup became lame. It was discovered that the pup had an orthopedic issue that is known in the breed: growth plates fusing too early. My friend was an experienced GSD owner. When the pup began showing signs of the issue and the breeder contacted, the breeder was totally unaware of the existence of the problem in her breed. However, a bit of research indicated that this problem was a common enough issue for which breeders need to be alert.

*****

The Abercrombies were a lovely family who had recently lost one of their beloved dogs. They knew they wanted a dog to not only be a lovely companion but also a possible Agility dog. They were well versed in Shetland Sheepdogs and worked to seek out a serious breeder. The breeder they chose worked hard to research backgrounds and pedigrees of dogs before breeding a litter. The breeder had invested a serious amount of money over the years in regards to testing, showing and then invested a lot of time preparing the puppies not kept for life outside her house. By the time the puppies not kept by the breeder went to new homes, they had begun learning to potty on different surfaces, had been exposed to various animals, sounds, situations, and people. They were learning to crate apart from littermates and other social skills. Each puppy came with a packet that included a contract, a few basic supplies, sheets covering the beginning things all puppies must learn and information on why early training is needed and how to find a good training program. They keep in contact with the breeder and the breeder with them. They have a lifetime friend and mentor in the breeder.

Again, it is up to you to research breeders and interview breeders, even if they get glowing recommendations from others. Use your gut. Good breeders will question you as hard as you should question them and steer you towards the best match based on evaluating you and what they have available. Serious breeders also network and can refer you to others who may have what you are looking for. For example, if you are looking at a retired show dog but have children, and the breeder tells you the dog has not been exposed to children, respect that. However, what if the breeder has a dog that was handled by a Junior Handler and has been proven great with children that is also available?   A serious breeder wants to make that placement permanent.

Be patient. A breeder may not have a puppy available immediately when you want one. It took me over a year to find my D'Argo. I knew various breeders. I let them know what I was looking for and stayed in touch. He was worth the wait.

PET SHOPS

Pet shops are convenient. Regardless of what a clerk or manager states, the bottom line, profit, is what drives them. From a business perspective, is it easier to sell an $800 puppy or enough supplies to equal that same amount? Even better, sell an $800 puppy PLUS $300 in supplies! There is incentive for those producing puppies for the pet trade to keep their costs down. Every extra cent put into the pups is profit lost. Some breeders for pet shops do put effort into what they do in regards to keeping cleaner facilities, needed vaccines, etc. but do they spend the hundreds or more in dollars on health screenings for breeding stock? No. Others do whatever they can to keep costs as low as possible. Puppies are sold to stores at wholesale cost, which can be significantly less than retail. The markups that are done with all goods are done with animals sold at retail. There is even less profit if the breeder goes through a broker to sell the puppies to stores.

Some store employees will tell you that they only use caring breeders. No really caring breeder will use a store or broker to place puppies. (Ask if you can contact the breeder to discuss what tests were done and see if you get the information you want). A good breeder wants to know exactly where the puppies are going. This is impossible to do through a pet store or broker. Another issue is that it is difficult to properly socialize and get pups a good start when in cages. Taking a pup from questionable background, in regards to health and temperament, and then dumping him in a store, can do even more damage developmentally. It is difficult to go into stores and see pups that have been there for weeks or months. Our hearts go out. However, should we mercy buy? The store managers do not care. All they see is an open cage for another puppy to come in. Pet shops do not care why pup is going; the clerk just made a sale and can now re-stock.

I remember one mom and pop pet shop when I lived in New England. It was a large store; they acquired stock through local, small commercial breeders for everything. It was also one of the most comprehensive pet supply stores at that time and the only one carrying the dog food I fed. (I eventually discovered a great feed supply store a few miles north, just over the state line carrying the same product). The puppies were kept in large, communal pens and segregated by size. There was always a staff member interacting with the pups and constantly cleaning the pens. It seemed great. However, the breeders they used were breeding animals with health issues. The majority of Dalmatian puppies sold were deaf. There were problem with diabetes in Maltese puppies. These were issues that were not visible upon purchase and that the required vet care before selling (vaccines) would not discover.

The storeowners wanted to get "better" (healthier) puppies to sell but none of the "show" breeders would sell to them. When I explained why they could not get puppies from the caliber of breeders they hoped for, the storeowners were shocked! However, I explained truly caring breeders have a lifetime interest in the pups they produce. They will not sell if they cannot have control over the homes where the pups are placed or be able to contract to have dogs returned if the owners found themselves in trouble and unable to keep the dog. I never saw the store staff refuse a sale to an owner not suited for a dog. I never saw the store try to talk a buyer out of a particular animal. I only saw staff push puppies and hundreds of dollars in supplies. I also knew people who purchased pets through the store and when crises hit, since the "return" period was over, the owners were stuck. Now this was supposed to be one of the best stores around to buy puppies. Yes, a person could go in and get a pup, but at what ultimate cost? Profit driven businesses are not thinking of the best interest of the animal or buyer, regardless of what you will be told. It is not in the best interest of a sales clerk to lose a store hundreds of dollars worth of sales either.

No matter how much you want a dog, your stand a better chance of getting a good match if you work with a well chosen rescue group or well-researched breeder. Do not fall into the trap of having to get a cute puppy or dog immediately. Impulsivity can lead to trouble.

CHAPTER FIVE

WHAT SHOULD I DO BEFORE I BRING MY DOG HOME?

Most dog owners are reactive and not proactive when it comes to bringing home a dog. It never ceases to amaze me the number of people I see at supply stores, with very young puppies in tow. The owners are in a panic because they never purchased any supplies before the fact. I receive many emails and calls from people rushing to find good vets and fast as they forgot that puppies need routine boosters or their dog was unvaccinated by the pound. Even worse, the pup came home, is very sick and the owner needs a cheap vet now. I also get calls from owners who are having issues and are in need of a trainer in their area as the dog has developed significant behavioral concerns. Part of readiness for a dog is being proactive. Before your new companion comes home, make sure you have all the supplies and contacts you need. Check out veterinarians and trainers and find ones with whom you are comfortable. If needed, line up a dog walker or day care well in advance before your new companion comes home. This chapter will introduce proactivity as opposed to reactivity.

BASIC SUPPLIES

What supplies should you have before your puppy or dog comes home? At minimum, you should have:

- Dog crate (if a large breed puppy, you can get a crate divider so an adult sized crate can be sized down then enlarged as the pup grows)
- Baby gates (at least two or three and order large ones should you have an open floor plan house)
- Bedding for the crate (you can use things from the house as well)
- Bowls (at least two and one for outside water)
- Food
- Leashes and Collars (I always have extra in case one gets chewed or outgrown)
- ID tag
- Various toys and chews for inside and outside use
- Plenty of clean up items

After your pet comes home, there will be more things you may need. However, if you have the basics ahead of time, it makes starting out easier!

FINDING A VETERINARIAN

Along with basic supplies, it is important to have a veterinarian lined up before your puppy or dog comes home. Even if the puppy or dog has reportedly been vetted prior to your acquiring, it is still important that you have a good veterinarian check the puppy or dog within 48 hours or less of coming home. Some contracts may require it. In addition, this gives a veterinarian a chance to get information on your new pet and meet you before an issue arises. I learned how vital an immediate visit is after adopting a kitten. I opted for a private rescue as I needed to make sure any feline I brought in had been tested for feline leukemia and feline immuno-deficiency virus as I have cats as well as dogs. I made this very clear to the rescue personnel and the foster care giver. I was assured all testing and vaccinations were done. The kitten was fine and healthy. My vet noticed that there was a discrepancy on the paperwork and what I was told. We tested the kitten and she was positive for feline leukemia. Sadly, the kitten had to be returned that night. When I called the foster care giver, she gave me a story about how you cannot test kittens. Had I waited the three weeks before she was due for another round of vaccines, my own pets would have been at greater risk. Had I known they do not test bottle-raised kittens at that rescue, I would not have adopted the kitten. Later, I learned from the foster care giver that the kitten was not a false positive, there was bone marrow involvement. The littermates tested similarly. Luckily, they did find a home together.

If you do not currently have a veterinarian you are using for other pets, a place to start is by contacting local rescues and ask who they use and why. Friends, relatives and dog trainers are good resources as well. If you are working with a local breeder, ask who they recommend. Once you get a list of names and clinics, go visit. Not all vets or clinics are equal. You need to find a vet that not only knows and is willing to continue learning his / her craft but also gets along well with you and your dog. Veterinarians need to go through continuing education; however, is that vet keeping up on things such as the new trends in vaccination schedules and research. Ask for references, credentials and any specialties the vet may have. Ask how they feel about the kind of dog you are considering. If you are adopting a dog with special medical needs, make sure your vet is familiar with the condition or can help you find a specialist who is.

Not only do you have to work with the veterinarian, but also various staff. How do you feel treated? Does the staff seem sympathetic and helpful or do they seem distracted? Does the staff seem relaxed with the animals or do they rush and grab? No matter how great a veterinarian is, if the staff is not equally as good at their jobs, the care your pet receives could be affected.

Other things to look for: does the clinic have overnight staff or will the animals be alone? Does the clinic offer other services such as boarding and grooming? Do they have regular hours that work with your schedule? What is your general impression of the facility? Can you tour it? Work with your gut instinct. If there is something that worries you, it is your right to ask about it. In addition, ask what will happen if there is an afterhours emergency? Is there a 24-hour clinic in the region or is there a staff member on call? Not all issues can or should wait until the clinic is open. Do all this before your new companion comes home.

A caller had purchased an older puppy several months earlier. The vaccines were done, and the owner assumed there was plenty of time before a vet had to be considered. Unfortunately, the dog had other ideas and she decided to eat a toy the day before I was called. Now she was vomiting seriously and it was a Sunday afternoon. The owner was having a tough time finding an open vet and had no idea where any emergency clinics were. He was resorting to calling dog trainers for help. Now, thirty seconds on the internet could have pulled up several emergency clinics – as I was speaking with the caller, I pulled out my laptop and did a fast search. The owner had not owned a pet before, was new to the area and had no idea of services he may need. Luckily, the dog did not have a condition like "bloat" which can be fatal in a short time.

FINDING A TRAINER

Along with a good veterinarian, a good trainer is an important ally. Sadly, many owners wait until a problem arises or is way out of control before seeking help. Even if there appears to be no issue, early enrollment in a class or a series of sessions with a private trainer at your home is a wonderful way to bond and help you learn to prevent common situations. A proactive dog owner working to prevent issues or who intervenes as soon as something worrisome starts, has a greater chance of making life with a dog work. Owners who wait too long have a greater likelihood of giving up their dog.

How do you choose a trainer? You must determine your needs in the beginning. Do you want a family companion, a competition companion or working dog? My personal opinion is all activities, formal or informal, begin with good manners. From there, you can develop specific behaviors for competitions or working. Therefore, for the new dog or puppy, a basic manners class that also teaches how to socialize is a great place to start. Find a trainer that starts dogs out at the bare beginning and will help evaluate your dog if the dog has had prior training. It is not fair to expect a child who cannot walk to ride a bike. Why should I expect a dog that cannot stand on a loose leash to walk on one?

When looking for a trainer, bear in mind that certifications, degrees and memberships ultimately only mean a person was able to pass the tests and have the money to go for certifications, degrees and memberships. These are things to look for but definitely NOT a guarantee the trainer is using the information needed to pass the tests. Many great trainers are not certified for legitimate reasons. Some of the most inhumane and questionable trainers out there have books published and have various certifications. Now what do you do?

It is easy to be blinded by trainers who own dogs with loads of competition titles. This also does not mean they are great trainers. It means they had the time and money to compete. The trainers may employ harsh techniques to get a dog to perform or they may not, you need to go observe and ask questions. In addition, competition training is not always practical for the average pet home. It can help, but unless the trainer is teaching you how to apply the lessons practically and understand why things such as training a formal recall exercise, as seen in competitions, is not a practical lesson or a home situation, you may not get the results for which you hope. For example, a competition style come when called or "recall" teaches a dog he has to hear "sit," "stay," then watch as you walk away, turn around and then come to you when called. What if you are outside with your dog and you spy a skunk before your dog does. You must call your dog away from when he is sniffing before HE sees the skunk? Will you really do the whole sit/stay/walk/call? No, you need a dog that will come without the chain of events prior to the desired behavior.

Finding a trainer may not be simple, there may be dozens to choose from depending on where you live – or there may be a scant few. In my area, there are honestly dozens trainers within a half hour of my zip code. Where a friend of mine is, there are two and a dog club within an hour. Again, you may want to start out with a trainer who teaches less formal and more practical lessons if your dog and you are just getting started. Check out organization such as the Association of Pet Dog Trainers and the International Association of Animal Behavioral Consultants for members in your region. Next, call and interview trainers. Ask about their background, types of dogs they work with, methods used for training, etc. A good trainer will know a variety of methods and find the most humane one for your dog's individual needs.

A few things to ask about:

- What materials are provided or do you need to provide? You should be provided with a leash and collar for group classes.
- Will the trainer work before or after class with you if needed? Everyone needs some one-on-one work at some point.
- Is there any form of written material to supplement the classes? You should not be expected to remember everything spoken and supplemental materials are a great help.
- If the trainer feels your dog is not suited for classes or is past the trainer's abilities, what provisions will be made? It is not fair or even safe for a dog not suited for group classes to be in them or for a trainer to take on something out of his/her range of learning. If the trainer is unable to work with your dog, can he/she teach you to manage the situation and help guide you to someone else?
- Does the trainer do a pass-fail? Pass-fail can be frustrating for humans. Dogs called flunkies are less likely to succeed in the home as the owners

begin to assume the dogs are unable to be trained. A good trainer focuses on the progress seen and keeps reminding the owner of successes. A good trainer is your cheerleader as well as your guide.

If you feel good about what you hear, ask to observe the trainer in action (this may not be possible if the trainer does only private work). You can ask for references but remember this: if an owner does not do his job out of class, the dog will not behave as desired, and who will be blamed? Chances are the trainer. Even great trainers will have students who were disappointed for one reason or another. The trainer may never find this out until a bad reference is given.

Other things to look for are:

- Small classes, there will be more attention to you and your dog.
- A trainer who does not tout him or herself as the best, no trainer knows it all or is suited for every student or dog.
- A trainer who will be able to refer you to others should the issues your dog has or develop are out of their range of experience at this point.
- A trainer with the resources to refer you to others for additional growth if you want to compete or create a working animal or who has advanced work in the areas you want.
- Look for classes that have the dog working at their own pace even within the same level.
- Look for a trainer who works well within the environment. No matter how great the environment (posh, state-of-the-art facility) if the trainer is ineffective, a great setting is nothing.
- A trainer who does not discriminate or refuse certain dogs based only on breed, a good trainer will research many breeds to give the best guidance they can.

A few red flags are:

- Trainers who guarantee their training. No trainer can do this. When you leave the class or when we leave the house, trainers have no control over what happens. Lack of work on the owner's behalf, lack of consistency on the family's behalf, not giving the dog what is needed, will affect results.
- Trainers who require membership into their "organization" or group in order to take classes.
- Trainers who state there is no dog he or she cannot train. There will always be a dog that, due to some horrible past event, fluke of heredity or medical condition, will not come around. The trainer just may not have met his or her biggest challenge.
- Trainers who insist you can only use one method to train. Remember, the ends do not justify the means in dog training. Immediate results may

look great, but is the trainer using leash corrections, ear pinches or intimidation to get results? Methods using force and intimidation can create more issues in the future.

A good trainer uses the most humane methods for the individual dog and owner. For example, clicker training is touted as very safe and humane. However, a clicker to a dog who is scared of the sound is a cruel training method. I have worked with dogs that could not tolerate the sound of the click. Trainers who state you cannot use food as a training tool may not understand how to use it to motivate and then wean it out. This is why trainers should use different, positive means. A good trainer will also know the pros and cons of each method, as well as, know the difference between training and masking a problem. For example, is that head halter really teaching a dog not to pull or is it making it difficult for the dog to pull? When on a regular, flat buckle collar, will the dog pull again? Will the trainer automatically put a choke or prong collar on your dog? A good trainer can make a world of difference. A bad trainer can make your job harder down the road.

Just because people are teaching classes, writing books or has/had a show on TV does not mean *they* are good trainers. It just means they are teaching, writing and got that media break.

What training programs are available?

There are three main categories of training I will discuss: group classes, private work, and board and train. It is important that you understand the pros and cons of each so you can make the best choice for you.

Group classes are probably the first thing dog owners think of when they think dog training. When looking for a group class, look for a small student to teacher ratio. Larger classes mean less attention to you. Even if the head trainer has assistants, each assistant will be slightly different and the class may lack consistency. I remember assisting in a class where I got great results with a huge, goofy Rottweiler with using just treats, fun and encouragement. No leash lunging or pulling, great focus, the dog was improving and the owner beginning to realize what a good he truly had. Then we rotated groups. The head trainer, now getting the Rottie's group, walked to the materials bin, pulled out a choke chain and told the owner that no Rottie can be trained without a solid correction. Within moments, the dog was cowering and confused. Next rotation, a different piece of equipment was used. I tried to speak to the head trainer but was ignored. I left the program after two cycles of classes. Ironically, I was asked to begin training with them after using the program to help socialize one of my dogs. The general club members wanted to bring in different ideas and more humane methods. Several club members knew I was also a trainer. Not one head trainer in the organization at that point was willing to change, so many of us left. That said, I have worked my dogs in group classes where assistants consulted with each other and the head trainer regarding individual dogs and how best to address training needs. If the program uses assistants, ask about how they are trained and what communication happens between them to help keep consistency for the students.

Group classes can be great for helping dogs learn to handle social situations and distractions while working in a controlled environment. A good puppy class should involve off lead play time if safe and encourage students to engage with each other's puppies. However, for a dog with poor social skills, fears or aggressions and/or an owner unable to manage the dog, group classes may not be suitable at this point. A good program will look at the individual dog, his needs as well as the safety of the class. If a trainer says your dog is not at this point suited for a group class, ask why and ask for a referral to a private trainer. Groups classes are often less expensive, but if your dog is not ready for group work, it is not fair (to your dog or the other students) nor safe to enroll.

Private training may be a good starting point for owners who: have not had a dog in a while: this is their first dog; dogs that are not ready for the stress levels of group sessions; dogs having issues that cannot effectively/safely be addressed in a group setting. With private sessions, you receive all one-on-one work and the lessons can be adapted to your particular needs. There are several things to look at with private sessions. If you are having issues in your home, will the trainer come there for sessions? The trainer should know the importance of observing the dog where the issues lie. Is there any evaluation at the beginning of the sessions? Does the trainer ask specific questions and ask you to write down a list of worries? What materials does the trainer provide? Can the trainer be contacted between sessions or after they are complete? Does the trainer give a wrap up with future goals outlined? Along with all the other concerns regarding dog training in general, you need to know what a trainer will offer you during private sessions.

Board and Train or boarding training is where you leave your dog and someone does all the work. This is often the most expensive as well as potentially the riskiest for your dog. What the trainer states will be done and what is actually done may be two different things. Shortly after I moved to Virginia, there was a "highly recommended" boarding-trainer in my region. The management claimed only to use positive motivation, food and fun. Unfortunately, the trainers were not using such methods. Eventually, worried kennel employees began to videotape events. The local news picked up the story. As each dog was pulled from his run, a prong or choke collar was placed on the dog. Leash corrections were used and there was very little praise let alone rewards. When the owners came back, suddenly the dogs were on buckle collars and being rewarded with food and games. Now, I need to say that there are good boarding trainers out there, but you need to choose very carefully. Ask if you can show up sometime without warning to observe sessions. If you are told no, then do not consider this trainer. There may be something hidden.

Some owners assume that boarding training will take the owner's work out of the equation. It does not. Once the dog comes home, the lessons learned have to be adapted for your environment. This will mean you will need to work with your dog to some degree. Another active regional program does use very humane methods in their boarding training. They take shelter dogs and use prisoners to rehabilitate the dogs and prepare them for homes. However, the people managing the programs were not preparing the owners or teaching how to transition dogs from the prison to the homes. Will the trainer come to your home, teach you what you need to know and do follow-ups? If not, no matter how good and humane the trainer, boarding training could be a waste of money. You need to be taught what to do in your home. I am not against boarding training; I am just stating this kind of training has the least control for the owner in regards to what happens once the dog is dropped off. Sometimes boarding training needs to be done such as training service dogs, but for the average owner, know the pros and cons.

Regardless of the program chosen, the cardinal rule of dog training should be the ends never justify the means if those means are harsh or painful. Training should be fun and motivating, firm when needed but never harsh, punitive or abusive. Programs advising scruffing, alpha rolls, leash-based corrections, prong collars, electric shocks, water sprays to the face, ear pinches (grabbing the base of the ear and tweaking, some owners call it the "Tch Tch!" like you see on TV – it is an ear pinch, hurts and can create a dog with hand-shyness) and such often do more harm than good long term. You cannot effectively bond or work with a dog if you are increasing his stress and anxiety. Most aggressions are reactions to stress, anxiety, perceived threats, and similar situations. Punishing the reaction may give a short term "cure" but worsen the problem as the dog's anxiety builds. Programs that include desensitizing (helping a dog overcome issues by introducing the stressor in small increments), counter conditioning (getting a dog to have a good association with a former stressor), and a lot of positive work should be sought out. This is not stating you cannot discipline a dog! I am stating it is what is done and how that makes the difference. Management of resources to increase or decrease certain behaviors can be more effective tools than a yank on a collar.

Once you find a trainer you are comfortable with, sign up for classes or sessions beginning as soon as possible after your puppy or dog comes home. Remember, even if there seems to be no problems, early intervention and training can prevent a host of issues in the future! A proactive owner who works to prevent issues stands a far greater chance of a long and happy life with a dog than one who waits for issues to happen and then reacts.

MISCELLANEOUS SERVICES

Any service you can see yourself needing, you need to look into before you are desperate to find help. Depending on what your individual needs are and those of the dog's are, this may include; dog walkers, day care, groomers, boarding kennels, yard clean up services. If you investigate options before your dog comes home, you have a better chance of getting a contract or appointment with a good business. Waiting until your dog comes home and then trying to find that extra service could cause you to choose someone inappropriate for the job. Knowing what you need and finding good people to work with you before your dog comes home will put you ahead of the game. The same concepts and approach to interviewing trainers can be used to interview groomers, sitters/walkers, daycares and yard services. Look for someone who is licensed in your area and insured.

When choosing a **day care**, look for one that uses crates to give dogs a break. Cage-free day cares are popular but if a dog needs a break and needs to get away he cannot in a cage-free situation. A crate gives a dog security and safety. He can rest without worry about being pounced on. A good day care will have various areas where dogs can be separated by age, size, activity levels, etc. It should be as clean as possible with employees cleaning and disinfecting immediately after a mess is made. The facility should not smell of animal waste. There should be things for the dogs to climb on, run through and play with. The fence should be at least six feet high and the entrance "air-locked" (door/gate with a "holding" spot and then a door/gate into the play area) so dogs cannot sneak out as others enter. You want to look for staff that appears attentive and constantly observing. If two dogs are getting rowdy and pushing the point of rough play and heading into possible fights, does the staff intervene? You also want to look for a good dog to staff ratio. No matter how attentive the staff, if there are too many dogs, the staff cannot as effectively monitor the dogs. If you see thirty dogs in a room with one person, leave. Also look for red flags such as stressed dogs being ignored. If a dog is acting up, is that dog given a break? Is he removed from the situation or is he held close in the middle of chaos (staff holding a stressed dog in the middle of chaos will increase the anxiety levels in the dog thus increasing the chance of a problem developing). If you are considering a dog day care that is out of someone's home, make sure the provider is zoned, licensed and insured for the business: one neighbor complaint could send clients scrambling to find a legal day care!

You may need a professional **groomer**. As with every service, ask people who they use and recommend. Visit the business and check for cleanliness, signs of stressed dogs and such. Just drop by and ask if you can see the building. How do you feel when you ask? What is the reply? Are you able to view the grooming area from the front desk? What do you see? How do you feel? Though I am not a huge fan of big box chain stores, I have always liked that the grooming is done behind a huge window, nothing can be hidden! Another idea growing in popularity are the do-it-yourself places. One place I personally use provides you with everything, there is staff to assist and I was taught to use professional dryers, clippers, etc. The staff at this one also does grooming with an appointment and the cost is far less. If you are lucky enough, there may be a mobile groomer in your area. These may cost a little more. Finally, make life easier for your groomer and ask your trainer to teach you to prepare your dog for being on tables, brushed, handled, etc. No matter how good a groomer is, if he/she cannot safely handle your dog, you may not be satisfied with the outcome. The groomer may even drop you as a client!

At some point you may need the services of a **boarding kennel**. Investigate kennels, talk to staff and patrons. Ask to look around the facility, the whole facility. Look for gaps in fencing where dogs may escape. Ask to see where foods and medications are kept. Ask how the dogs are exercised. If the dogs are walked in an unfenced area, ask if the staff double leashes the dog to help prevent escape if a leash breaks or is slipped off. If the dogs are in a communal pet for play time, how many staff members are observing the dogs? How are the dogs grouped together? What if your dog is intolerant of others dogs, what will happen? Ask if you can stop in for an unannounced visit of the facility. Will the dog be bathed before pick up? Is there 24 hour monitoring of the dogs? Be wary if you are not allowed to investigate a certain area or there are areas set aside for inspections. There may be a reason why people are not allowed in other areas (lesser quality care is one). How does the staff seem with the dogs? Are they calm or do you see anyone doing things like yelling at dogs to shut up or kicking runs to forcibly quiet the dogs. Is the staff trying to calm stressed dogs by giving them things like stuffed bones or toys meant to have food stuffed inside? Are the kennels and play areas clean? When dogs relieve themselves, is it left there or cleaned up quickly? In case of emergency, what will happen? If the person is boarding out of their home, is the business properly zoned, licensed and insured? There was a situation locally where a woman was caring for others' dogs along with having quite a few of her own as well as fostering for a rescue she was involved with. This woman was not zoned or licensed for what she was doing and was many times over the legal limit for dogs. People complained about the noise and smell. The county authorities tried for some time to get her to comply with the law. She refused and eventually all animals on her property were confiscated.

With a **dog walker**, look for one who is licensed and insured. Ask if they walk the dogs or take them to a local dog park. Dog walkers who take a group of dogs to a park are creating a liability. I had a client who told their dog walker not to take their dogs to dog parks. One of their dogs would not tolerate other dogs getting in her face. The walker ignored the owners, took the dogs to a local dog park and there was a fight when a strange dog barged up to her. Also beware of those who will also train your dogs. I had a dog with which I had done extensive work. I knew the owner used a dog walking service. We started seeing problems we had worked out of the dog returning. I asked the owner to have a neighbor observe the new walker. Come to find out, the new walker was also apprenticing with a dog trainer. She was using her walking services to train client dogs (without telling the client) as practice. My client asked her to cease that as it was undoing our work. She also called the business she was working with and said if it persisted, the contract would be terminated. The dog walker ignored the dog owner and lost a client for her business. If you are working with a trainer and using a dog walker, make sure the walker is on the same page as you and the trainer. Dog walkers provide an important service but could also do harm if you do not carefully choose the person you employ.

Any service you may think you will need, investigate and make your choice before your puppy or dog comes home. Think of these services as you would any supply you would need for your dog. The better prepared you are, the better off you will be.

CHAPTER SIX

SPECIAL NOTES ON SPECIAL NEEDS DOGS

Every now and then, someone looking for a dog sees or hears of one that does not just tug at but rips those heartstrings. I have adopted special needs animals in the past. It can be very rewarding but also extremely taxing on the owner. Acquiring a special needs dog takes not only all the prior considerations but additional thought regarding the individual issue(s) with the dog. No matter how badly you feel for that dog, you must step back and think with your head. I break down special needs into three major categories: behavioral, physical and medical. There may be overlapping of any or all categories.

BEHAVIORAL

Many people give up dogs due to "behavioral" issues. Sometimes the dog is really not a significant behavioral issue. Instead the dog was not getting what was needed in the previous environment in regards to training, manners work, mental and physical activities. Some dogs may have concerns that need extra work but can still be brought around to become wonderful companions. Sometimes the dog is truly a significant danger, has a biting history, the owners were warned by authorities about the dog, etc. The dog may be extremely fearful to the point of chronic panic (fearful dogs are a greater biting risk if they decide that escape is not an option.) The owner cannot bear to put the dog down. They take the dog to the local pound or decide to place him through online lists. Sometimes the issues are a result of genetics. Nature gives us the basis of temperament. We nurture that into desired behaviors. If nature does not give us much to work with, there is only so much behavioral modification can do.

Make sure you are willing and able to devote the time and money needed to rehabilitate a dog with behavioral issues and if it becomes apparent that you have done everything possible that you are able to make the tough decisions.

Spud was a very typical specimen of his breed: small, active, inquisitive, willing to work. He was a rescue and had been through some rough times in former homes. His current owners knew what the former homes had done to Spud. They knew he was a special needs dog in regards to behavioral issues. His owners had Spud for several years and had no idea how to work with a dog with fear aggressions. One trainer insisted on an electric shock collar that would be triggered every time Spud aggressed. To add complications, they now had a preschooler and an infant. Stress levels rising, Spud began biting "with no reason or warning." Well there was a reason: Spud was consistently expected to deal with severe anxiety-inducing situations without any positive work. Spud increased his reactions because he was associating the punishment coming with the presence of the things of which he was afraid. (If child enters the room and starts to yell, I will be hurt, therefore I must keep child out of the room). Too add to the situation, Spud was getting nowhere near the physical and mental work outs he needed. After months of work and environment changes, Spud had come around phenomenally. Things that before would trigger a growl and nip, Spud handled well and would actually look for a cookie instead of his old reactions. I knew he was well on his way when the oldest child accidentally bumped into Spud as the child jumped off a climbing toy. Spud raced to the husband, sat and waited for praise. A month earlier, Spud would have snarled at the child. Spud was associating the older child with good things; her tantrums were no longer triggering negative reactions. Spud had learned to walk away.

After a few more weeks, the owners decided they did not need any more work and I was very pleased with where Spud was behaviorally. We did a wrap up and future goals session where I explained carefully that these changes have to be kept up and the new change be for Spud's life, keep up with the counter conditioning, desensitizing and management instructions and do not go back to the old ways. I gave them resources to give Spud safe outlets for his energy. I was promised by the wife that she would continue the work. I asked the couple to report back in a few weeks to see how things were going. I did end up returning to tweak a couple things with the oldest child and remind the mother about the need to stay on course. Spud was still doing well and I was happy. I felt as long as the owners did what was working this home could work.

Then the call I always dread: months later, Spud had begun attacking "without provocation." Back to the house I went. The wife had not kept up with what was working and admitted to the husband she liked her old ways. It was easier to yell and spank than reinforce good manners for the child. The child was back to hitting Spud. The wife was back to punishing Spud. To add to the risk, instead of exercising Spud with walks and the fenced area her husband erected, she was now allowing him to run loose. No legitimate rescue would take him due to liability. They were considering sending him to the local pound and not telling employees the truth why Spud was being surrendered. Small, cute dog, he would be scooped up by a family in a heartbeat if he did not show his returning aggressions in the shelter. Owner surrendered dogs are often put right on the adoption floor unless there are concerns. Spud was a very dangerous dog at that point and not a candidate for adoption due to his fear aggression. Luckily for Spud, he became one of the very rare dogs to be adopted by a behaviorist but it took a lot of work to find one willing to adopt him and accept all liability. Imagine what would have happened if Spud ended up in the shelter and placed in a new home?

When considering adopting a dog with behavioral issues, you need to think long and hard about this. Ask questions: who evaluated the dog, how many times and can you see the results of each evaluation? What many call temperament testing in actuality is just an evaluation of the behavior seen at that given moment time. Many factors can cause a dog to do poorly and fail a test. I evaluated a dog with the potential to be a good pet for a quieter home. However, he had a severe case of entropion (inverting of the eyelids causing the lashes to irritate the eye). I felt he would have evaluated better if he were not in pain. This dog was hurting but tolerant and inquisitive. My recommendation was have the entropion corrected and re-evaluate. It was not a major surgery and one the local vet who diagnosed the dog had done many times.

Overzealous evaluators or ones who do not understand the limits of evaluations are second concern. Dogs that have been beaten with sticks may react adversely to a fake hand on a stick being thrust in his food bowl. A dog barking and lunging at another dog may not be dog aggressive but just have misinterpreted, poor social skills. Alternatively, the dog may be aggressive and the evaluator thinks he is just excited. Temperament testing (more accurately, behavioral evaluations) is somewhat controversial in the world of dog training and rescue. Do not discount the evaluations; just realize they are only as good as the evaluator. With some dogs, this may be the only information you have. If considering a dog with behavioral concerns, ask a trainer not affiliated with the group to look at the dog with you.

Travis was a stray. Animal control had worked for over three months to catch the terrified dog. Travis was then transferred to a local breed rescue. He was scared and his foster mom called me for some help. In seven months, Travis went from backing away from humans to seeking them out. Travis was doing well in increasingly stressing situations, beginning to enjoy visitors, Travis would willingly give up things he had, he was handling travels and really becoming a wonderful dog. Travis was worked with privately and in small group settings. He still needed work but I was optimistic that with a little more time, Travis would be ready for adoption into an adult-only home. The rescue coordinators called a different trainer to evaluate Travis because they wanted him adopted sooner. The rescue coordinator was instructed by the other trainer to put him down as a dog that would never be able to be placed. I knew the other trainer and how aggressively she evaluated. I read the report and saw photos of Travis during the evaluation. The report was that Travis did not care for humans and should be put down. The evaluator had no first hand, long-term knowledge of Travis. She took no history. She had no idea how far he had progressed in and out of his foster home. Nor did she take into consideration that the test was done in a very stressing environment (her dog day care facility) and was administered quite aggressively. The foster care giver said she was in tears as she watched as Travis was bullied, poked with sticks, grabbed and jabbed, lunged at by the dogs used for evaluating his reactions towards strange dogs, etc. He never snarled or snapped, he just backed away. Luckily, Travis suffered no long-term effects from the aggressive evaluation and rebounded wonderfully. Eventually he found a home and was exceeding everyone's expectations.

If you have any doubts about your ability to bring in, manage the dog safely while putting in the time or effort and expense to attempt to bring about the dog, do not take the animal.

Bringing in a dog with serious behavioral issues could be the difference between literally life and death. Think: you adopt a dog with known possession issues. You have to step out of the room while the dog has his favorite toy or is on the couch. Your small child wanders up and gets too close to the dog. The dog reacts strongly and seriously mauls your child. Most good rescues will carefully place dogs. However, not all will or even can. (Go back and read the section on rescue groups). On occasion owners who acquired dogs through a free list contact me. Often a sad story was given about how no rescue would take the dog and the dog will be put down because the owner does not have the time for the dog so they are placing the dog by using an online listing. The person who saw the ad became so upset that he/she had to do something. Sometimes the dogs were not taken by a private rescue because the issues were too significant and posed a real risk. Instead of being responsible and putting down a dangerous dog, the current owners decided to down play the issues and "adopt" the dogs out themselves. You need to be very careful when searching these lists. Just because we want all homeless dogs to have a warm fireplace and loving hand, there may not be a home suited for the dog with severe behavioral problems. Not all dogs can be safely and sanely rehabilitated to the point where they can live safely and sanely within the average human house or community. This is just the sad fact of irresponsible dog owners and their willingness to pass on problems to others after refusing or whatever reason to work with the situation in a meaningful way.

Before you adopt a dog with known behavioral issues, ask yourself:

- Can I safely, sanely and humanely manage these issues while I find someone to assist me?
- Can I ensure the safety of those in the home and around me while I work with the dog?
- Can I afford the expense and time to attempt to work out the issues including medical testing?
- Can I make any and all environmental changes recommended to ensure safety while I work with the dog?
- Am I willing to alter my life to fit the needs of the dog as indicated?
- Am I willing to accept legal responsibility for anything my dog does?
- Am I willing to consider euthanasia and not pass the issues on to another if it is determined that this dog is too dangerous and I know I cannot resolve the situation?

Rehabilitating a behavioral special needs dog is rewarding. However depending on the issues and the severity of them and / or underlying factors, taking on a behavioral issue dog can be heartbreaking and even dangerous.

Angel was adopted through an online "free" list. Her owners could no longer keep her, and gave a great sob story about how they could not afford to train her. A kind soul adopted her but fast found out that Angel, as just a wee pup, was exhibiting severe aggression issues to other dogs and showing signs of human aggression. Her adopter was worried that the former owner lied.

*****

Alice came to her new home with several known significant fear issues in place. Luckily the new owners knew what happened in her first home. This was a big help to me as I could better create a plan of rehabilitation. The owners devoted every moment possible to rehabilitating Alice. At the end of our sessions, Alice's owners were comfortable with the exercises and ready to fly solo. Several months later, I received a wonderful email. Alice was now travelling all over the country and even preparing for her first long boat ride (owners have a luxury boat), had no fears, greeting people and was a spectacular companion. I have to admit that she was a dog I had worries about. The damage done to Alice was significant and well known. She had shock collars used and had developed serious collar fears. She was hit, socially neglected and just extremely fearful. Alice was also a HIGH energy cross expected to live a low energy life. Then her new owners came along. They went into Alice with eyes open and rational expectations. Alice went from a dog terrified of everything to one who enjoys outside dining, meeting and greeting and travelling.

PHYSICAL

I define this as a dog that is: blind, deaf, missing a limb, chronic lameness due to birth defect or injury, neurological issues, etc. Dogs do not react to physical handicaps as humans do. I am always amazed how dogs can adapt to things that may cause severe depressions in humans. The accommodations you need to make will depend on the type of physical issue the dog may have. For example, a dog missing a leg often manages just fine, especially if you keep the dog in good physical shape. Dogs with hearing or vision impairments may startle faster and require changes in how they are greeted such as a verbal cue for a blind dog or a sensory one like a set of taps on the floor for a deaf dog. Dogs with neurological issues that affect movement may need environmental accommodations made.

Before you bring in a dog with a physical disability, you need to research the disability and decide if you can make needed accommodations. You also need to make sure you can afford any surgeries or physical therapy, trainers, etc., the dog may require. Dogs with physical disabilities are adaptable and can live full, wonderful lives.

Sometimes the dog is fine upon purchase or adoption. Below is such as example of a dog that was sick upon entering the home but not so into the illness the symptoms were easily visible and the illness resulted in permanent damage. This dog illustrates just how well she learned to cope:

Pip was a pup purchased from a local breeder who was churning out "designer dogs." Shortly after coming home, Pip showed signs of having the devastating Parvovirus. Due to the incubation period and timing, it seemed safe to assume the issue was contracted at the breeder's. Pip was a lucky pup to survive Parvo. However, it left her mostly blind and with neurological damage affecting movement in her hind legs. Her owners made the commitment to Pip and decided to keep her. Over the weeks, Pip learned to navigate the house and yard. She learned scents and signals alerting her to things she may bump into or fall down both in and out of the home. The owners learned how to teach her stairs and how to manage curbs. It was not going to be easy for her owners; however, they made the needed accommodations and were serious about providing a safe home for Pip. Last time I saw Pip, unless someone looked closely, it was almost impossible to tell Pip had any issues. However, Pip will always need closer watching and people have to be wary not to just touch her without warning.

*****

Sassy came into a rescue group and was in rough shape. She had a severe leg injury that required amputation. Sadly, the rescue was very short on funds and paying for the surgery was going to be difficult. Luckily, a person who was willing to accept the costs of not only the surgery but also adopting Sassy was found. After having her leg amputated, Sassy went on to attend training classes and to accompany her owner to various events as a demonstration dog.

*****

Jasper was a large dog of a breed where deafness due to uneducated breeding is common (in some breeds, breeding certain colors or patterns to the same color or pattern is to be avoided, he was from what is called a double merle or merle to merle breeding). His owner never let that stop him. Jasper was not a client of mine but was adopted by a trainer at a facility where I used to volunteer and take various classes. Last time I saw Jasper, he was successfully navigating an Agility course in preparation for competition.

Physical issues can worsen behavioral concerns. A deaf or blind dog may startle or nip quicker if startled. If you remember this and employ a few safety steps like tapping the floor in a specific pattern or calling the dog's name to signal what is going to happen can prevent startles. I have worked with deaf and blind dogs and they do make great pets. A dog with limb deformities or spinal issues who is in pain may have lower tolerance to things and need pain management. Dogs missing a limb really do not care, they generally do fine if you keep them in good physical shape. If the situation is properly managed, the dog can live years as a happy, fun-loving companion.

MEDICAL

Medical issues with dogs can be short term or long term. As with behavioral and physical issues, you need to look at the medical concerns and determine if you can afford and live with the problem. Some issues like ear infections, a damaged tail needing amputating, serious dental work required or parasitic infection may require a short run of treatments with a short-term investment in time and money but have no long-term effects. Other medical issues may last the lifetime of the dog and require constant medicating. Epilepsy, diabetes, Cushing's Disease, heart conditions, hydrocephaly, etc, are some medical conditions that often require lifelong treatment and possibly increased veterinary visits. As with all medical issues, it is your responsibility to manage financially and emotionally the condition. It is sad how many pets wind up back in rescue when adopters failed to consider the costs. Often the heart overrides the brain and people just feel they must save the dog.

Please note that behavioral issues might have a basis in health. Going back to the dog with entropion I evaluated. The dog was shy but did show recovery and curiosity to various stimuli. I could not help but think his eyes; the discomfort the condition was creating, was playing into the dog's behavior. The dog had vision but his eyes were inflamed. I could not do a decent evaluation of the dog as long as the medical issue persisted. However I was seeing enough in the dog despite the condition that I felt comfortable recommending correcting the eyes and reevaluating when the dog was healed. Sadly, the rescue coordinator opted to put him down.

If you are looking at acquiring a dog with physical or medical concerns, ask if you can have the dog examined by an independent veterinarian and trainer for your choice before finalizing the adoption. You have the right to get as much information about the condition(s) the dog has before you permanently take on the dog.

Mason suffered from seizures and some behavioral issues when he entered rescue. The new adopter knew this. Mason was being managed quite well with phenobarbital upon intake to the rescue. The foster care giver (also who would be choosing what applicant would adopt Mason) decided that seizures were best treated with diet and pulled him off all medication just before adoption. The seizures returned shortly after adoption. The new owner called the foster care/adoption counselor who said it was most likely dietary. The adopter was instructed to feed a specific diet and Mason would be fine. The seizures returned within days. The foster owner/adoption counselor told Mason's new owner to go holistic and recommended a vet who would not use any "chemical drugs" to manage the seizures. When holistic treatment failed, it was decided Mason needed to be back on medication. He was put back on phenobarbital and did well. The foster care giver recommended finding a new vet. This vet changed his meds again to a newer drug that had fewer long term side effects to the liver. This new medication controlled the seizures but created behavioral issues. A well-documented side effect humans reported was increased anxiety. Mason would pace and circle uncontrollably around the couch. Within a few weeks, he had worn the finish off the floor. Mason would pace until he passed out from exhaustion. He could not manage any behavior modification for the other issues he came into the home with and since the pacing behaviors were triggered by the new drug, modification would not be that effective on that. The vet refused to change Mason back to what was working. So another vet was found and yet more medication trials.

Mason's owner went through thousands of dollars in veterinary expenses from medications to a veterinary neurologist at the end (he passed at the neurologist's clinic). This does not even account for the emotional stress on his owner. Sadly, Mason was euthanized. After months of pain and stress, Mason went into a series of seizures from which he never came out. The sad thing was; Mason was doing well with the first medication. The foster owner decided to pull him off them without medical consult because she did not like having dogs on medications. I can only wonder if the outcome would have been different had this not happened and he been allowed to stay on the phenobarbital. Even sadder, after his loss, the rescue group tried to get Mason's adopter to take his sister, who guess what... also suffered from seizures. Mason's adopter did not get all the information she needed regarding Mason, nor did she think to ask questions about how he was being treated prior to adoption and why the Phenobarbital was stopped.

*****

Neelix was adopted by me, though not a dog, Neelix illustrates the importance of research and serious consideration with medical issues. Neelix was born in a shelter. His mother was one of over five dozen purebred cats confiscated from a local person who was breeding Himalayans and Persians for the pet store trade. All the cats had ringworm. Dozens of kittens were born at the shelter while the case was going through the courts. Neelix was medically the worst. Along with one of the worst cases of ringworm the shelter and my vet had ever seen, he was born with a massive hernia. It took months of care and thousands of dollars to save Neelix. Many people and several rescues stepping in to rescue the cats once the courts gave custody to the county. Most of the cats were returned to the shelter for severe behavioral problems and the high expense of medical treatment. Several years later, I was speaking with and animal control officer who had been present at the raid. Of the dozens of cats and kittens taken or born at the shelter after the raid, Neelix was one of maybe five or six who had a favorable outcome. Before adopting Neelix, I knew what I would be getting into. I knew his ringworm could take months to resolve, the hernia would be a relatively significant surgery due to its size and due to the need for isolation during ringworm treatment, I knew I may have behavioral issues to content with.

Many people did not do their homework and dashed out to save the cats, only to *return them to the shelter when it was realized that the cats would need extensive time, money and work to rehabilitate. I have to say, that Neelix was one of the most tolerant, sweetest cats with whom I have ever shared my life. The time and effort was well worth it. I lost Neelix shortly before publishing this book. He had inherited polycystic kidney disease. PKD is known in Persians and related breeds, there is a genetic test for it. When Neelix was twelve, he went into renal failure. We spent months supporting him until it was time to say goodbye. PKD is nothing a rescue would have picked up and can take years to show symptoms.*

Adopting special needs animals is rewarding but should never be entered into without serious thought. If you are not capable of managing and/or working through and/or with the issues, the results can be devastating. Some special needs are very easy to work with while others can drain the bank account or prove to be dangerous to you and the community. No matter how we feel about the special needs pet, if you are not able to do the work, it may be best to choose an animal better suited to what you can handle.

CONCLUSION

In my field, I often see the results of dog owners who put careful thought and choice into their companions. These owners asked questions, researched and made certain everything was in place. Let me share with you some success stories. These people looked at themselves and what they could offer a dog before bringing one home. They researched the source of the dog and were patient. When a potential owner does all possible to prepare for a dog long before the event happens, they begin what may be some of the best times of their lives.

Hilda and Matilda were two sisters of a respectable age. They wanted a dog and acquired one that was suited to their physical abilities and capabilities. Though retired, they were still very active in their community. When they started having a few minor issues with Clara, I was called in before things got out of control. Within a few sessions, Clara was much improved and her manners back under control. However, had Clara been a different dog, larger, more energetic or younger, things may have been much different.

*****

William and Kathy were a middle-aged couple, no children and they had a few physical issues between the two of them. When they chose their dogs, they went with a breed they knew suited them and worked with good sources. Their newest dog, Scamper, was a handful. Though knowledgeable and experienced owners, Scamper was a lot of dog even for the breed. I worked with them to adapt training to the physical abilities of the humans. I also gave them suggestions for working with Scamper's activity levels. Though physically neither owner could keep up with Scamper, at my suggestion, they took him to a local Agility club's classes, just for fun. Another club member, who was a trainer, saw Scamper playing on a course, and fell in love with his desire to work, she began competition training with Scamper. Years later, William and Kathy are busy running behind the scenes things for the Agility club. Scamper is a lovely companion at home with Kathy and William but a fierce competitor in the hands of the other club member. Had William and Kathy not found someone who could help give Scamper what he needed, they all would have been miserable.

*****

Missy was taken from friends of the Burkes. She was still more pup than adult (even at well over 100 pounds) and in a bad state. Missy feared certain articles of clothing (anything with a hood that was up) and was very confused. Within the first week of coming home, I was contacted. Other trainers had told them to give it time and Missy would eventually settle in. Not always and dogs do better when they are worked with from the moment they enter the new home. The Burkes wanted to prevent issues from happening and resolve the ones Missy came with. It was determined Missy had more energy than anyone expected, especially for her breed. The Burkes' work schedules were longer than suitable for Missy's individual needs. After some manners work, Missy was a regular at dog parks (all her issues were human-based and those were resolved) and loving a new day care. By the end of our sessions, Missy was a far happier and saner dog in her new home. However, had the Burkes let things go and followed the blind advice of others (who never asked to evaluate Missy), Missy could have become a very risky venture. A bit of forethought, the ability and willingness to make needed changes to meet Missy's needs made a world of difference.

*****

Timmy was an impulse buy. His owners had researched dogs, learned from experts where to find a dog and what to look for; however, they were sucked into a pet shop pup. Timmy was from a highly questionable background and his "registration" papers turned out to be from a bogus registry (one created by the pet shop breeder industry to give false credibility). Within forty-eight hours of purchase, he was sick. Luckily, it was nothing life threatening. It was also discovered his vaccinations were given when Timmy was too young therefore considered ineffective. Additionally, he was riddled with parasites though the records from the facility stated he had been regularly tested. The owners thought they were getting a bargain. Timmy had been at the store for a couple months. He was no longer a darling, sellable pup so the owners were given a "deal" on him. Nevertheless, by the time his owners finished paying for all the little "additions," they could have purchased or adopted a healthier pup from a more reputable source. The owners recognized the mistake they made and were willing to do what was needed to get Timmy back on the road to recovery.

Determining your preparedness for a puppy or adult dog, type, source and long-term ramifications of pet ownership is a serious undertaking. Sadly, too many people put more consideration into what type of car they want than they will when acquiring a living creature. Sometimes the best dog owner is the one who realizes he/she is not ready for a dog.

Be responsible and think before you act: when humans do some research and think things through before getting a dog, the chances of a long and happy relationship increases.

RESOURCES

American Kennel Club
5580 Centerview Drive, Raleigh, NC 27606
www.AKC.org

United Kennel Club
100 E. Kilgore Road, Kalamazoo, MI 49002
www.UKCdogs.com

Canadian Kennel Club
89 Skyway Avenue, Suite 100
Etobicoke, Ontario M9W 6R4
www.CKC.ca

PetFinder
www.PetFinder.com

Association of Pet Dog Trainers
www.APDT.com

International Association of Animal Behavioral Consultants
www.IAABC.org

American Veterinary Medical Association
www.AVMA.org

American Boarding Kennels Association
www.ABKA.com

National Dog Groomers Association of America
www.nationaldoggroomers.com

National Association of Professional Pet Sitters
www.petsitters.org

Dog Wise, resource for ordering various dog books and videos
www.dogwise.com

RECOMMENDED AUTHORS

There are too many superb authors to list them all. Here are a few I have found quite informative over the years and frequently recommend to my clients.

Dr. Ian Dunbar
Dr. Patricia McConnell
Jean Donaldson
Karen Pryor
Turid Rugaas
Dr. George Padgett

www.ingramcontent.com/pod-product-compliance
Lightning Source LLC
Chambersburg PA
CBHW071309040426
42444CB00009B/1941